CHRISTIANITY AT THE CROSSROADS

Combining expansive storytelling with striking analysis of "networks, nodes, and nuclei," David N. Hempton's new book explains major developments in global Christianity between two communication revolutions: print and the internet. His novel approach (replete with vivid metaphor – we read of wildflower gardens and fungi, of exploding fireworks sending sparks of possibility in all directions, and of forests with vast interconnected root systems hidden below our vision) allows him to look beyond institutional hierarchies, traverse national and denominational boundaries, and think more deeply about the underlying conditions promoting, or resisting, adaptation and change. It also enables him to explore the crossroads, or junction boxes, where individuals and ideas encountered different traditions and from which something fresh and dynamic emerged. Cogently addressing the rise of empires, transformation of gender relations, and demographic shifts in world Christianity from the West to the Global South, this book is a masterly contribution to contemporary religious history.

DAVID N. HEMPTON is University Distinguished Service Professor and Alonzo L. McDonald Family Professor of Evangelical Theological Studies at the Divinity School, Harvard University, where he also served as Dean from 2012 to 2023. An internationally acclaimed religious historian, he is the author of numerous books focused on the early modern and modern periods, several of them award winners. His publications include *Methodism and Politics in British Society, 1750–1850* (Hutchinson, 1984), which in the same year won the Whitfield Prize of the Royal Historical Society, *Religion and Political Culture in Britain and Ireland: From the Glorious Revolution to the Decline of Empire* (Cambridge University Press, 1996), *Methodism: Empire of the Spirit* (Yale University Press, 2005), *Evangelical Disenchantment: Nine Portraits of Faith and Doubt*

(Yale University Press, 2008), and *The Church in the Long Eighteenth Century* (I. B. Tauris, 2011, winner of the 2012 Albert C. Outler Prize of the American Society of Church History). He has delivered, over the course of his career, several sets of endowed lectures, including the Cadbury Lectures at the University of Birmingham, the F. D. Maurice Lectures at King's College London, and the Gifford Lectures at the University of Edinburgh, from which the present book is derived. He is, in addition, a Fellow of the Royal Historical Society, a Fellow of the Ecclesiastical History Society, and an Honorary Member of the Royal Irish Academy.

This important book will have a broad appeal to lecturers, students, clergy, and a larger reading public. Hempton directs particular attention to those dissatisfied with things as they are, those disenchanted with formal institutions, settled churches and traditional practices, and seeking new dispensations – those for whom this worldly life is and must be a pilgrimage. He explores a number of networks and voluntary associations, both formal and informal, which have transformed Christianity. They include Protestant Reformers and Jesuit missionaries, Catholic pilgrims in Mexico and the United States, freed Black slaves in Sierra Leone, Pietists, Methodists, premillennialists and Pentecostals, women Protestant missionaries and Catholic women's orders, and the "religious digital creatives" of the new digital age. He shuns a Eurocentric historical narrative that portrays beliefs and values as being transmitted from a Western center to a non-Western periphery, or from the Global North to the Global South. Rather, he seeks through his "networks, nodes, and nuclei" approach to show that there have been multiple world "centers" in Christian history, and that cultural influences move from the Global South to the Global North, as well as from North to South. His stimulating book, clearly written in an engaging style, reveals exciting new paths for future research.

**Stewart J. Brown, Professor Emeritus
of Ecclesiastical History, University of Edinburgh**

A skilled narrator, David N. Hempton offers a new approach to the history of modern Christianity. The focus is on the means by which new religious ideas were disseminated to wide sections of the population in previously Christianized regions of the world and new Christian communities formed, or by which Christianity became established and won a popular following in new territories. Hempton's main interest is in the role of transnational networks, and he is especially concerned to go beyond the roles of governments, ecclesiastical hierarchies, or denominational leaders, vitally important as these often were. His "from below" approach is especially apposite in the earlier stages of movements which may later be more fully institutionalized and controlled. The author is one of the leading historians of modern British, Irish, and American religion. He has published on many very different topics, and his work is notable for his broad sympathies as well as the range of his knowledge. Here he succeeds in his declared aim of steering a middle path between the reductionism of many social and political historians and the uncritical enthusiasm often offered by denominational historians. He provides empathy and a serious attempt to understand what the actors in his stories believed, while at the same time remaining always alert to the constraints as well as the opportunities arising from their social and political context.

Hugh McLeod, Emeritus Professor of Church History, University of Birmingham

David N. Hempton is one of a handful of historians of Christianity whose expertness runs all the way from the sixteenth to the twenty-first centuries, and whose scope is truly global. *Christianity at the Crossroads* is a stunning addition to the literature. Why do I say this? First, the breadth of the reading that has gone into this volume is breathtaking. The author clearly has read deeply in primary and secondary and tertiary sources. Indeed, I cannot think of any other historian of Christianity (with the possible exception of Peter Brown) who commands all three genres as he does. Second, his prose is consistently clear, straightforward, and often quotable. The text is not burdened with religious or social studies jargon of any sort. Though the book is not perhaps beach reading, any reasonably educated student of the subject at the college, seminary, or doctoral level will find it accessible. The Barnes and Noble browser will find it engaging too. Third, he advances an argument that is, to my knowledge, distinct if not unique in the field. A few scholars have presented learned gestures in that direction but only Hempton has carried it through with a systematic, comprehensive, fully documented vision of the whole. Finally, the book is simply deeply interesting. Anyone with a reasonable curiosity about how Christianity in the West has acquired the amorphous, vibrant, sometimes dangerous yet often also life-giving shape that it has today will find compelling answers in a truly landmark work.

Grant Wacker, Gilbert T. Rowe Distinguished Professor Emeritus of Christian History, Duke University

CHRISTIANITY AT THE CROSSROADS

THE GLOBAL CHURCH FROM THE PRINT REVOLUTION TO THE DIGITAL ERA

DAVID N. HEMPTON

Harvard University

CAMBRIDGE
UNIVERSITY PRESS

CAMBRIDGE
UNIVERSITY PRESS

Shaftesbury Road, Cambridge CB2 8EA, United Kingdom

One Liberty Plaza, 20th Floor, New York, NY 10006, USA

477 Williamstown Road, Port Melbourne, VIC 3207, Australia

314–321, 3rd Floor, Plot 3, Splendor Forum, Jasola District Centre, New Delhi – 110025, India

103 Penang Road, #05–06/07, Visioncrest Commercial, Singapore 238467

Cambridge University Press is part of Cambridge University Press & Assessment, a department of the University of Cambridge.

We share the University's mission to contribute to society through the pursuit of education, learning and research at the highest international levels of excellence.

www.cambridge.org
Information on this title: www.cambridge.org/9781009597432

DOI: 10.1017/9781009597449

First published 2025

Printed in the United Kingdom by CPI Group Ltd, Croydon CR0 4YY

A catalogue record for this publication is available from the British Library

Library of Congress Cataloging-in-Publication Data
NAMES: Hempton, David N., author.
TITLE: Christianity at the crossroads : the global church from the print revolution to the digital era / David N. Hempton, Harvard University.
DESCRIPTION: Cambridge, United Kingdom ; New York, NY, USA : Cambridge University Press, 2025. | Includes bibliographical references and index.
IDENTIFIERS: LCCN 2024054934 | ISBN 9781009597432 (hardback) | ISBN 9781009597449 (ebook)
SUBJECTS: LCSH: Church history. | Missions – History. | Ecclesiastical geography. | Christianity – Forecasting.
CLASSIFICATION: LCC BR145.3 .H368 2025 | DDC 270–dc23/eng/20250212
LC record available at https://lccn.loc.gov/2024054934

ISBN 978-1-009-59743-2 Hardback

For Hadleigh and Emma

CONTENTS

PREFACE

Over the course of its 135-year history, the Gifford Lectures have been delivered by scholars with deep ties to Harvard University – including Paul Tillich, my colleagues Diana Eck and Steven Pinker, and, of course, William James, whose classic study *The Varieties of Religious Experience* started out as Gifford Lectures. It is a great honor to continue in this rich tradition and to be able to contribute the perspective of a historian to the distinguished ranks of philosophers, natural theologians, and ethicists who have given these lectures in the Scottish universities, where I started my own academic journey some fifty years ago.

In the chapters that follow, I have tried to retain some of the flavor of the lecture format, with its more direct style, summary judgments, and provocative conclusions, while adding a more traditional scholarly apparatus of introduction, conclusion, notes, bibliography, and index. On a few occasions, I have also drawn on previous work, partly to show the evolution of how and why I began to think of the analytical structure behind what follows. I hope the notes in some way pay tribute to the generosity and creativity of other scholars who have helped me along the way, including the Cambridge University Press readers, whose comments were invaluable.

My last introductory remark comes from a private letter from Jane Ellen Harrison (1850–1928) to Gilbert

Murray, Regius Professor of Greek at Oxford in 1915. Harrison was raised as an evangelical Christian and became an eminent classicist and theorist of religion. She was the first ever research fellow at Newnham College, Cambridge. Gilbert Murray was also an eminent classicist, and he had just turned down an invitation to deliver the Gifford Lectures, most likely for health reasons. Harrison was very disappointed for him and for herself. She wrote, "You see there are only two people who are scholars & with literary minds who understand that these things [mythology and religion] are at the back of everything ... The specialists don't count – they grub up the facts but don't see the relations."[1] I quote this partly out of self-protection, knowing that trying to say something fresh about 500 years of Christianity, from the Reformation to the present, is going to disappoint specialists who know much more about some of the periods and places than I do, but I hope to show that the "relations" or, in the parlance of this lecture series, the "networks" and the connections, are beneath the surface of many things that we thought we knew about.

[1] Letter to Gilbert Murray. Nov. 8 [1915] Box 2, page 15. Jane Harrison Collection, Newnham College Archives, Cambridge. The letter is quoted at length and discussed in Annabel Robinson, *The Life and Work of Jane Ellen Harrison* (Oxford, 2007), pp. 214–15. I am grateful to my former colleague Meryl Winick for this reference and for her generous support of this lecture series and book.

ACKNOWLEDGMENTS

As anyone who has ever been asked to give a distinguished set of lectures knows very well, feelings of joy and a sense of honor quickly give way to dread and angst. In my case, the invitation to deliver the 2021 Gifford Lectures in Edinburgh took me to the extremes of both of these feelings. Joy was compounded by the fact that I had started academic life as a doctoral student at the University of St. Andrews, just up the coast from Edinburgh University, where coincidentally my wife was a student. Dread was compounded because I accepted the invitation while holding the position of Dean of Harvard Divinity School, a position that left little time for research and writing. My first acknowledgment, then, is to the then President and the Provost of Harvard, Larry Bacow and Alan Garber, who granted me a semester's sabbatical leave. My second debt is to my colleague and fellow historian, David Holland, who took on the position of interim Dean of Harvard Divinity School with cheerfulness and immense professionalism.

Scholarship at its best is a collaborative venture, especially when traveling, historically speaking, to times and places way beyond one's own expertise. I am especially grateful to my colleagues at the Divinity School for reading drafts and saving me from even more egregious errors than the ones that remain. These include Ann Braude, Catherine Brekus, David Carrasco, Frank Clooney,

David Hall, Kevin Madigan, Michelle Sanchez, and Todne Thomas. I am also delighted to acknowledge the help and stimulation of cohorts of graduate students who took classes with me on the subject of this set of lectures. Special thanks go to my doctoral students, Helen Kim, Tom Whittaker, and Kelsey Hanson Woodruff, whose ideas and help with research have made an immeasurable contribution to this book. I owe a special debt to William Taylor, who imparted, with remarkable generosity of spirit, some of his vast scholarship on the Iberian empires to a novice, and to Grant Wacker, who read the drafts of all six lectures and corrected some of my inadequate understandings of Protestantism and Pentecostalism in the United States and beyond. Emma Anderson likewise imparted much needed wisdom from her expertise on the Catholic missions in New France.

To complete the manuscript, I benefited from a writing fellowship from the Rockefeller Foundation at the Bellagio Center on Lake Como in Italy, graciously hosted by Pilar Palaciá. My wonderful fellow residents put up with too many conversations about the history of religion, while they were engaged on more life-and-death projects, and feigned interest way above the call of duty. Their names are inscribed in the Bellagio book of life: Walid Ammar, Dave Chokshi, Natalie Diaz, Rob Epstein, Kelly Gallagher, Darrick Hamilton, Nikole Hannah-Jones, Ayana Johnson, Claire Leibowicz, Hiroya Miura, David Sklansky, and Michael Webber. I also received generous support from Peter McDonald and the McDonald Agape Foundation.

My greatest thanks are due to the faculty, staff, and students at Edinburgh University, who could not have been more hospitable and also proved to be expert and deeply engaged interlocutors. I am especially grateful to Jay Brown, Alvin Jackson, Susan Hardman Moore, Brian Stanley, Mark Newman, Emma Wild-Wood, Dorothy Miell, and the indefatigable Victoria Turner, whose expert lecture summaries and blog postings were a constant source of delight.

Many others, too numerous to list, have contributed to this enterprise, but perhaps it is fitting to end with a heartfelt acknowledgment to those who helped me start out on this academic journey almost half a century ago and without whose stimulation and support nothing would ever have been accomplished. These include Sheridan Gilley, the late John Walsh, and the late W. R. Ward. It has also been an enormous pleasure working again with Alex Wright at Cambridge University Press, whose friendship and belief in this project has sustained me through many revisions.

Last, but far from least, my thanks, as always, go to my family who joined me for the lectures – Louanne, Stephen, and Jonney – and to our wonderful new additions – Christina, Hadleigh, and Emma.

Introduction

~

Old provincial society had its share of this social movement …
those less marked vicissitudes which are constantly shifting the
boundaries of social intercourse, and begetting new consciousness of
interdependence … Municipal town and rural parish gradually made
fresh threads of connection.

George Eliot, *Middlemarch*

This book emerged from an invitation to deliver the
2021 Gifford Lectures, which were endowed more than a
century ago to "promote and diffuse the study of Natural
Theology in the widest possible sense of the term."[1] That
was an intimidating task to me as a mere social historian
of Christianity who has often worked at the interstitial
margins of religious traditions so often conceptualized
within national, denominational, institutional, and hierarchical categories on the one hand, and established spatial and conceptual boundaries on the other. My starting
point was to frame the subject of the lectures between
two communications' revolutions – print in the early
sixteenth century and digital media at the turn of the
twenty-first century – and to try to tell a new story of
religious change based on transnational networks and
junction boxes (or nodes) of encounter where new and
unpredictable energies were unleashed.

[1] "The St Andrews Gifford Lectures." https://gifford.wp.st-andrews
.ac.uk/.

I also looked upon the lectures as an opportunity to open up a conversation about ways of writing religious history, specifically around the inescapable tension between telling stories and exploring theories and methods, which are sometimes regarded as inhospitable rivals. The eminent Italian photographer Paola Mattioli concisely framed this in her own work as a tension between the "narrative and the conceptual" – story and theory – which can open up bigger questions about social and political structures as well as honest reflections on the conscious and unconscious perspective of the gazer or the writer.[2] In this way photography seeks to capture both some form of representational "truth" and also convey a fresh way of seeing and experiencing the familiar and the unfamiliar.

Similarly, in the writing of any kind of history there is an unavoidable tension, creative at its best, between narrative or storytelling on the one hand and conceptual or methodological framing on the other. This book is both an attempt to tell transnational stories about some of the most significant developments in the history of Christianity over the past five hundred years and an exploration of a method framed around the alliterative concepts of nuclei, nodes, and networks. The nuclei are the inner DNA, or memes, of religious ideas which

---

[2] Paola Mattioli, Commentary for an exhibition at the Villa Carlotta, Lake Como, 2022:

If I have to sum up my position on photography, I can say that I've chosen to stay on two planes. One narrative and one conceptual. As for the narrative, I prefer stories that contain strong thematic nodes in themselves. This often leads me to important topics, of social and political commitment. I have called the second aspect conceptual ... which in turn cannot ignore the theme of seeing. It is the gaze that questions what I am doing.

enable them to be transmitted way beyond their point of chronological and geographical origin; nodes are places of encounter, collision, fertilization, and reconceptualization where new possibilities are imagined and new energies unleashed; networks are the channels of transmission, which are sometimes physically and structurally obvious, and sometimes hidden from conventional viewpoints as tunnels are from surface maps. These networks are usually superimposed upon other connecting structures in symbiotic relation with one another.

Two other influences shaped my focus on nuclei, nodes, and networks. The first is a lifelong fascination with what I regard as one of the greatest works of English fiction, *Middlemarch*, written by George Eliot, who was not only a novelist, but also a distinguished philosopher, intellectual, and interdisciplinary thinker. In the quotation heading this introduction, Eliot is reflecting on the nature of social change, ostensibly in nineteenth-century England, but later universalized with a reference to Herodotus. Her view is that old social structures seem superficially solid and irresolute, but "fresh threads of connection" and demographic mobility subtly erode them and produce something new.[3] *Middlemarch*, subtitled "A Study of Provincial Life," is a sophisticated fictional treatment of how those "threads of connection" work in social relationships and structures. Eliot relentlessly uses web imagery to recreate the complex connectivity of any human society, and her employment of network imagery in the context of mid-Victorian England is breathtaking in its scope. In her efforts to penetrate the hidden structures of

---

[3] George Eliot, *Middlemarch*, Book 1, Chapter 11, paragraph 3.

3

Middlemarch society, she analogizes about the connectivity of human nervous systems and cholera epidemics, railways and telegraphs, village gossip and communication threads, spinning and weaving, underground rivers and growing vines, economic dependencies and the power of money, and even the construction of knowledge and language themselves.[4] The central point of the novel is to show that any human life is shaped and molded by a bewildering range of networks and social forces, some seen, but most largely unseen. My argument in this book about the spread of new religious ideas and movements and the erosion of older ecclesiastical patterns is similar.

A second influence is that these Gifford Lectures, now book chapters, were mostly written during the Covid-19 pandemic, which consciously and unconsciously reinforced in my mind this theoretical model of nuclei, nodes, and networks. In the pandemic, what was the virus (or nucleus core) that was being transmitted? What were the nodal junction boxes and networks of transmission, both surprising and unsurprising? And what does the spread of anything, from ideas to viruses, tell us about underlying social and political structures that transcend national boundaries and established ways of thinking? Apparently, the coronavirus that caused Covid-19 first appeared in Wuhan, China, spread to the Chinese provinces primarily through rail networks, then appeared in Italian cities, other Western European sites, and the United States. Air travel, tourism and professional networks, and close

---

[4] For a fuller treatment, see Laura Otis, *Networking: Communicating with Bodies and Machines in the Nineteenth Century* (Ann Arbor, MI, 2001), Chapter 3, "The Webs of Middlemarch."

human interactions in large cities all helped spread the virus from a single site to large parts of the globe.[5]

Over time, therefore, I came to see the "natural theology" prompt of the Gifford Lectures as less of a fear to be overcome as an opportunity to be embraced. Perhaps dangerously for someone who thinks too much in terms of metaphors and pictures, I came to think of my methodological framework of nuclei, nodes, and networks in terms of pictures from the natural world – of spiders' webs, dendritical root systems, and flowing rivers – all images that emphasize mobility, connectivity, and complexity. As the project unfolded, one particular image proved to be most helpful. I became intrigued by the potential of the metaphor of mychorrhizal fungi, which are thread-like fungi that have a symbiotic relationship with plants, drawing energy down from the plant's photosynthesis above ground and sending up essential nutrients from underground. The Royal Horticultural Society defines mychorrhizas as "fungal associations between plant roots and beneficial fungi. The fungi effectively extend the root area of plants and are extremely important to most wild plants, but less significant for garden plants where the use of fertilisers and cultivation disrupts and replaces these associations."[6] Translated into the religious changes that are the subject of this book, I am more interested in the "wild plants" of networks that are mostly not sponsored by nation states, ecclesial institutions, or denominational

---

5 For a recent, provocative account of how outbreaks of infectious diseases have shaped human cultures and societies, including the rise of Christianity, see Jonathan Kennedy, *Pathogenesis: A History of the World in Eight Plagues* (New York, 2023).

6 "Mycorrhizal fungi," RSS. www.rhs.org.uk/advice/profile?pid=633.

hierarchies, but are generally more spontaneous and have unintended but creative consequences. Such an approach pays more attention to change from below and to actors and contexts that often do not surface in the established literature. To write this way is not to mount an attack on excellent historiographical traditions focusing on established churches and national religious traditions, nor is it to presume, mistakenly, that there are no important connections between those traditions and the stories I am telling.

I am aware of the various dangers and limits of such an approach, which I will consider more intentionally in Chapter 1. Inevitably, it helps us understand change better than continuity, success better than failure, novelty better than conventionality, and impact better than stagnation. In other words, wildflower gardens seem more exotic and colorful than those tended by gardeners determined to create order, maintain control, and suppress weeds. Moreover, the wilder the garden, the more likely it is to be overtaken by invasive and nonindigenous species capable of disrupting preexisting ecosystems and causing a great deal of harm. It is one thing to celebrate the popular religiosity that springs from the margins; it can be quite another to live with its consequences.

Moving from the metaphor to the subject itself, it is still largely the case that historians of Christianity, even when innovative in theory and method, have mostly written within national, denominational, or institutional frameworks. Yet many of the most significant changes and developments within Christianity have been transnational in scope, trans-denominational in character, and not easily contained within institutional or hierarchical structures. What difference would it make, therefore, to reimagine the history of Christianity in terms of transnational networks, nodal junction boxes of encounter and transmission, and a greater sense of the core memes and messages of religious traditions and expressions? Those are the principal questions to be explored in the following chapters.

Chapter 1, "Towards a Theory of Transnational Religious Change," will define the terms (nuclei, nodes, and networks), explain the choice of dates between two revolutions in communication (print and the internet), and give some concrete historical examples of the tangible benefits of looking at the history of Christianity through transnational flows and networks. This approach allows us to cross national and denominational boundaries and borders, and to think more deeply about the underlying social and cultural conditions promoting or resisting adaptation and change. It also enables us to explore the crossroads or junction boxes where religious personnel and ideas encountered different traditions and from which something new and dynamic emerged.

Chapter 2, "Religious Networks in the Reformation Era," looks at two networks that transformed the early modern world. The first was the Iberian network of discoverers, conquerors, and missionaries that helped usher in an age of European world domination and colonialism. The second was facilitated by a new technology, printing, which helped unleash the huge religious and political disruption we know as the Reformation. What Niall Ferguson calls a "religious virus that came to be known as Protestantism" disrupted an ancient ecclesiastical hierarchy, fractured into many pieces Europe's

Catholic Christianity, and ushered in a long era of violent conflict.[7] This chapter will investigate religious networks within the Lutheran, Reformed, and Radical wings of the Reformation and highlight the formation, evolution, suppression, and ultimate survival of the Jesuit Order as a classic transnational network within Catholic Christianity.

Chapter 3, "Religious Networks in the Age of Empire in New Spain and Africa," is an attempt to explore the colonial era foundations of two of the most striking developments in the modern history of global Christianity, namely the respective strengths of Catholic Christianity in Central and Latin America and of Protestant and Pentecostal Christianity in mostly sub-Saharan Africa. The chapter aims to shed light on these important stories by focusing on two early modern, imperial case studies, one from the Spanish conquest of New Spain and another from the British colonial project in West Africa, specifically Sierra Leone. To what extent does our theoretical model of nuclei (the inner core of religious traditions), nodes (points of connection and exchange), and networks (transnational flows of people, ideas, and artifacts) help us understand better the various processes that produced such significant consequences for the global transmission of Christianity in the early modern and modern world?

Chapter 4, "The Protestant International: Pietism, Premillennialism, and Pentecostalism," seeks to understand some of the most significant developments in the English-speaking Protestant world in the last four

---

[7] Niall Ferguson, *The Square and the Tower: Networks and Power, from the Freemasons to Facebook* (New York, 2018), 87.

8

centuries, including the transition from pietism to evangelicalism, the explosive growth of Protestant missions, the origins of premillennial dispensationalism and its contribution to the rise of American fundamentalism, and finally the worldwide spread of Pentecostalism. None of these developments in the creation of a "Protestant International" can be studied within a single denominational or national tradition and none can be understood without coming to terms with its nucleus of ideas/theologies, the nodal points of its transmission and dissemination, and the transnational networks that facilitated its growth.

Chapter 5, "Women's Networks: Opportunities and Limitations," aims to address the reality that most religious traditions and movements have majorities of women, but most are led by men and are based on deeply embedded patriarchal assumptions. That underlying paradox is played out in multiple different Christian traditions and shapes the subsequent contests for power, representation, and influence. This chapter is animated by a primary question from which other questions naturally flow: What are the characteristics of the religious networks constructed by women and to what extent do they function differently from those built largely by men? In attempting to answer that question, I will identify five distinct kinds of networks, representing different varieties of female leadership and participation. It is important to state that this typology should not be read necessarily as either an ascension or declension narrative about women's agency and the role of patriarchy in shaping that agency.

Lastly, Chapter 6, "'Only Connect!': Christianity in the Digital Age," poses the questions: How is Christianity changing in the age of social media and international connectivity? What social and cultural changes were already underway in the decades immediately preceding the internet revolution that have a direct bearing on the generations most affected by that revolution? What is the impact of new technologies and social media on the beliefs, practices, and "lived religion" of Christian communities, organizations, and denominations? Finally, to what extent has the internet helped develop global religious networks in which the directional flows of power and influence have begun to change from a North/South trajectory to the reverse, or to lateral flows from South to South both across and within continents.

I will try to define concepts and terms clearly in the first chapter, but before reading further, it is important to signal a few cautions. The first is that institutional networks, or networks that have preserved institutional sources, for example, the Society of Jesus and pre-denominational Methodism, leave larger documentary trails and are consequently better studied than informal networks which may have multiple dispersed nodes of power and multidirectional channels of transmission. The latter are harder to uncover but are often surprisingly influential and underestimated by archival historians. Second, it is important to recognize that it is an unfortunate part of the colonial legacy that historians located in Europe or North America are simply better at understanding flows of religious influence and energy moving from North to South and East to West than the reverse flows from South to North or within the Global South. This is a longstanding and generic problem, but it has increased in global salience over the last century along with the dramatic demographic shift in the respective strengths of world Christianity between North and South. More and more books are appearing, especially on sub-Saharan Pentecostalism, showing that nodal centers of African Pentecostalism that were once receptors of a bewildering variety of primarily American influences are now vigorously exporting a distinctive form of African Pentecostalism to other sub-Saharan countries, and increasingly to the rest of the world.[8]

The importance of this point for understanding what is happening, and what will happen, in world Christianity, and how it is going to be interpreted, should not be underestimated. Over the course of the twentieth century, Christianity experienced a remarkable demographic shift. In 1900 around four-fifths of Christians lived in Europe and North America, whereas by 2000 around two-thirds of all Christians worldwide were living in the Global South (following the United Nations' definition encompassing Asia, Africa, Latin America, and Oceania).[9] It is vital to recognize that interpreting this dramatic shift cannot be done adequately from a Western vantage point, and that the nuclei, nodes, and networks involved in this transformation will be different from what they were in the past. So part of the rationale for this book is not only to construct a theoretical lens through which to explain changes over the past half of a millennium, but also to offer a

---

[8] For an excellent example, see David Maxwell, *African Gifts of the Spirit: Pentecostalism & the Rise of a Zimbabwean Transnational Religious Movement* (Oxford, 2006).

[9] I am grateful to Gina Zurlo for this reference. See the information collected and presented by the *World Christian Database*, currently located at Gordon Conwell Theological Seminary.

framework, necessarily shorn of Western hegemony, for understanding what has happened over the past century and what will happen in the decades to come.

One final caution is for us to be aware of the dangers of using network and nodal terminology, including homogenizing a religious movement and/or flattening out its unruly contours in search of its essence. One way of doing so is to lighten up on theory and prescription and tell *stories* with nuance and a sense of complexity. That is what the photographer, Paola Mattioli, was getting at in her reflection on her own method. Like her, I have chosen to stay on two planes, one narrative and one conceptual, in the hope that the former will represent the central point while the latter involves gazing, interpreting, and conceptualizing within rich social, economic, cultural, and religious contexts. As with any theory or method utilized in the study of the past, the test is whether or not it aids understanding and introduces new ways of *seeing*. It is now time for the test.

I

Towards a Theory of Transnational Religious Change

~

The initial idea for this book came from two unrelated events. The first was a conversation with the late distinguished sociologist of religion, David Martin, who offered the suggestion that a potentially creative way of looking at the history of Christian transmission over the past 500 years is to focus on nodal points of religious and cultural exchange when preexisting religious traditions intersected with one another and something new, dynamic, and energetic emerged from the encounter. Two examples came immediately to mind. The first was the melting pot of religious traditions in continental Europe and the British Isles which encountered one another in London in the 1730s, specifically in the Fetter Lane Society, which contributed significantly to what historians have labeled the First Great Awakening. Martin also thought that the history of Pentecostalism, about which he had just finished writing a book, was amenable to a similar interpretation, including the Azusa Street episode itself. In the following chapters, I plan to introduce many other nodes or junction boxes that have substantially altered the shape of global Christianity over the past 500 years.

The second idea came from an invitation to deliver a plenary address at a conference of British–Scandinavian church historians on the theme of "International

Religious Networks" held at the University of Lund in Sweden in 2005. I chose to speak about the rise and international spread of popular evangelical traditions, especially Methodism. Although I had worked on those traditions for many years, I had never before thought of them as classic religious networks. My main argument was that the historiography of Methodism in Britain and America had been dominated by how Methodism fitted into larger questions of national significance, such as the relationship between religion, social class, and revolution in Britain, and slavery, race, and the rise of a market economy in the United States. These are all important questions, but they do not say much about how exactly Methodism transcended national particularities and its English point of origin to become a transnational religious movement that expanded right across the world. Yet the more I thought about it, the more obvious it became that Methodism was indeed a transnational network that was not sponsored by any state or church, was not backed by significant political or economic resources, and owed little to the penalization of its rivals or adversaries. It was a classic network, even organized as such, with its itinerant preachers, classes, circuits, conferences, and constant mobility. Methodism was literally a federation of religious societies in connection with Mr. Wesley, which in turn were subject to the rules and regulations of the network, freely entered and freely left. Information flowed up and down the networks, from centers to peripheries, in the form of annual conferences, a formidable book and tract publication enterprise, and movement of personnel – locally, nationally, and transnationally.

The symbiosis of a Methodist structure that was built for mobility and an international order of unprecedented population movement was a particularly crucial factor in the rise of Methodism from an English sect to an international movement. From the sugar plantations of the Caribbean islands to the trading routes of the East India Company, and from the southwestern migrations of enslaved Americans to the convict ships bound for Australasia, Methodists exploited the mobile margins of trade and empire, establishing societies as they traveled.[1] Equipped with a flexible ecclesiology that easily facilitated expansion and armed with a sense of being part of a growing international movement, Methodism was highly mobile. The Methodist laity, identified by their ubiquitous class membership tickets, which functioned as both religious passports and abbreviated letters of recommendation, could change their location without changing their religious tradition. The much prized tickets containing the date of the foundation of the Wesley Methodist Society (1739) and a little scriptural verse was both an entrance pass into the quarterly meeting love-feasts and a network access card.

Other papers delivered at the conference on international religious networks showed the potential of network analysis in many different areas and periods of religious life, including medieval saints' cults, monastic

---

[1] David Hempton, *Methodism: Empire of the Spirit* (New Haven, 2005); Dee E. Andrews, *The Methodists and Revolutionary America, 1760–1800: The Shaping of an Evangelical Culture* (Princeton, 2000), 35–38; William John Townsend, George Eayrs, and Herbert Brook Workman, *A New History of Methodism*, Volume 2 (London, 2018), 237–81; Ian Breward, *A History of the Churches in Australasia* (Oxford, 2001).

orders, Reformation ideas and personnel, transatlantic Anglicanism in the age of empire, ecumenical, women's, and missionary movements, and much else. Drawing all this together, the editors of the conference volume suggested that religious networks could be formal and informal, metaphorical or actual, centripedal or centrifugal, based mostly on ideas or personnel (or both), and sometimes reified existing structures of power and influence and sometimes challenged them. All this shows that the concept of networks is an especially expansive and potentially slippery one, but that does not mean it should be avoided, especially if it means that the writing of religious history would remain dominated by either denominationally or nationally specific historiographical traditions.

The primary questions raised by the Swedish conference remain germane: "How far has religion, both in terms of the ideas it creates and in terms of its practitioners and adherents, been especially good at forming international networks? If so, what is it about religion that gives it such leverage and such an ability to transcend national and regional boundaries and divides?"[2] What is a network and how do religious networks differ from, say, religious movements? What are the advantages of using the concepts of social and religious networks as

[2] Jeremy Gregory and Hugh McLeod (eds.), *International Religious Networks (Studies in Church History, Subsidia)*, Volume 14 (Woodbridge, 2012), xx. For examples of attempts to use network theory to explain the transmission of religious ideas in even earlier periods than those covered by this volume, see Greg Woolf, "Only Connect? Network Analysis and Religious Change in the Roman World," *Helade* 2:2 (October, 2016), 43–58; Anna Collar, "Network Theory and Religious Innovation," *Mediterranean Historical Review*, 22:1 (June, 2007), 149–62.

distinct from more conventional denominational or institutional histories? Conversely, what are the potential disadvantages of organizing thoughts around the concept of religious networks? Are there built-in biases of which we need to be cognizant? For example, is it possible that networks focus disproportionate attention on male social elites and entrepreneurs who can write, organize, publish, and travel? Put another way, is this a way of revitalizing elite intellectual history, or are there ways of guarding against that narrowing of focus? Given our contemporary fascination with networks and social media, are there real dangers of exporting anachronistic categories into previous centuries? Since much of the early work on network theory was done by sociologists, including an influential cell at Harvard, what is the relationship between sociological and historical approaches to networks? Does theoretical model building help or hinder contextual analysis based on time and place? All these questions merit attention.

So what is a religious network and how do we define it in ways that are precise but flexible, clear but not limiting, and above all avoid the danger that the "concept will become malleable to the point of vacuousness"?[3] My working definition is that a religious network is a group or system of interconnected people, ideas, or spaces designed to achieve a religious purpose beyond the confines of existing borders and boundaries established by states, hierarchies, or religious traditions. Hence a network is

---

[3] Kate Davison, "Early Modern Social Networks: Antecedents, Opportunities and Challenges," *American Historical Review*, 124:2 (April, 2019), 456–82.

distinct from a movement because of its evident intercon-
nectedness, and is distinct from an institution in terms of
its fluidity and mobility, though over time many networks
may, and frequently do, become movements, adopt institutional characteristics, and create durable structures.
Using networks as a primary metaphor and tool of analysis is a way of drawing attention to religious mobility
and otherwise undetectable processes without necessarily
undervaluing more conventional approaches to the study
of religion. I want to be clear at the outset that my main
interest in looking at historical change through the prism
of networks is not primarily to get into definitional wars
about the respective merits of descriptive nouns – whether
networks, movements, nascent structures, or whatever –
but rather to draw attention to the fact that the study
of religious change and innovation is often limited and
even falsified by the imposition of rigid analytical categories and boundaries such as denominations, nations, and
organizational hierarchies. I will give some concrete historical examples later in this chapter.

What, then, would it mean, asks Manuel Vásquez

to study religion in ways that acknowledge national and
regional histories, the impact of the state, and the power of
religious institutions in imposing orthodoxy while taking
into account transnational, global, and diasporic processes
and recognizing the pervasiveness of religious flows and creativity? What kind of metaphors can we deploy to study religion *in motion*? Thus far, three clusters of metaphors have
emerged: spatial metaphors including terms such as landscapes, maps, territories, fields, geographies, cartographies,
and place-making through dwelling and crossing; "hydraulic"
tropes such as flows, fluxes, confluences, currents, and streams;

and models of relationality and connectivity like networks, webs, and pathways. Like the global, transnational, and diasporic modalities of religion, these three clusters of metaphors are not opposed to each other.[4]

In this way networks can help explain "mobile religion's flexibility, mobility, connectivity and innovation, without ignoring how it is often implicated in the hard realities of exclusion, exploitation and subjugation, which are also part and parcel of globalization."[5] Applying computer science network theory to religious networks, I will suggest that networks are mostly sustained by flows of information, personnel, and images, but these flows are not unidirectional, nor do they remain unchanged as they move from centers to peripheries and also in reverse. To state the obvious, the speed of transmission and change depends upon the technological sophistication of the information flow and the social and political structures within which they operate. For example, internet technology facilitates change faster than print, and empires facilitated international transmission faster than individual nation states. Similarly, religious institutions based on fixed territorial units such as ecclesiastical parishes are less amenable to rapid dissemination than those based on more mobile and less spatially dependent religious traditions, though they can operate as effective facilitators of state policy and propaganda when needed.

A node, according to one dictionary definition, is a point at which lines or pathways intersect or branch: a

4 Manuel A. Vásquez, "Studying Religion in Motion: A Networks Approach," *Method & Theory in the Study of Religion*, 20:2 (2008), 165–66.
5 Vásquez, "Studying Religion in Motion," 179.

central or connecting point. It can also be defined as the point on a plant stem when two or more leaves emerge, which speaks to growth and fertility. In terms of religious transmission, nodes are often places where people, ideas, and movements intersect and produce something different or more fertile. Obvious nodal points in religious transmission are universities, cities with intersecting, migratory populations, imperial distribution centers, and media hubs. In the history of Christianity, some nodes were carefully orchestrated and planned, such as the Council of Trent or the Hampton Court Conference, while others are more haphazard or unanticipated, but perhaps even more significant. My focus will be on the latter. The last of my three framing words, a nucleus, is the positively charged center of an atom or the very heart of a group or a movement. Translated into religious terms, what is at the heart-and-center of religious networks that supplies the energy to effect change? To give concrete examples, what was the meme of Methodism that supplied the coherence and energy to its rapid transnational growth? One contender for this central idea is a strong optimistic belief in the achievement of personal and social holiness on earth as in heaven. Over the course of the book, I will ask comparable questions about the Protestant Reformation, the Jesuit Order, Latino Catholicism, evangelicalism, fundamentalism, and Pentecostalism.

Defining the word "network" only gets us to the starting line. Other questions quickly follow. What do networks consist of? How do they arise? How do people, ideas, and material objects move along networks? How do our metaphors and pictures shape our conceptualization of how networks operate? For example, do some networks function dendritically, like the limbs, branches, and twigs of a tree, implying directionality from a center to a periphery? This concept inevitably privileges geography and can lead to the assumption that communications and change are channeled spatially from metropoles to distant colonies. Below ground, trees offer another picture of a natural network. It turns out that trees communicate with each other through a complex underground network of thread-like fungi, called mycorrhizae. Through this network, trees share resources such as carbon, nitrogen, and water. The resources flow down concentration gradients. Younger trees benefit from more mature trees and different species symbiotically share an ecosystem which allows all of them to withstand stress, drought, and other destructive events.[6]

Are other networks more like electricity grids, where all parts are interconnected and always have intersecting junctions? This concept privileges nodes or junction boxes and focuses attention on the intersections. Still others may be pictured as concentric circles that can be set in motion, as with a stone in a pond. This concept privileges the initial point of energy, or nucleus, and then how the ripples generally move from an epicenter to distant points, but rarely return. The point is that the concept of networks is particularly open to visualization and diagrammatic expression, which in turn shape the analysis, both helpfully and unhelpfully.

---

[6] Colin Tudge, *The Tree: A Natural History of What Trees Are, How They Live, and Why They Matter* (New York, 2006).

One reason that this subject appeals to me as a social historian of religion is the recognition that religious networks, particularly successful ones, depend on geological deposits of network-friendly soil that allow some networks to flourish almost parasitically on other social changes from which they benefit but do not create. For example, Methodist networks could not have thrived in the British Isles and across the Atlantic without preexisting conditions created by networks of Anglican parishes, expanding empires (including mobile armies), Pietist population migrations, and transportation innovations. Methodism was a classic association born in the age of associations and it benefited from the social and economic conditions that allowed it, along with other associations, to flourish. As we shall see, the same pattern holds true for most religious networks, even if the social conditions change with time. Successful religious networks depend for their success on preexisting social conditions that facilitate their transmission. Put another way, networks do not stand apart from culture, nor do they take the focus off time and place, nor do they necessarily stand against other kinds of social analysis based on hierarchies and existing structures of power.[7]

As with any theoretical or methodological tool applied to religious history, the proof of its utility is whether it allows us to see new or more accurate dimensions to familiar stories, or perhaps even to open up new fields of enquiry altogether. Here are two brief concrete examples to get us started. The first comes from a recent article in *Church History* and carries the title "A 'Syncretism

[7] Davison, "Early Modern Social Networks," 475.

of Piety': Imagining Global Protestantism in Early Eighteenth-Century Boston, Tranquebar, and Halle."[8] The essay examines a network centered on the Boston Congregational minister and theologian Cotton Mather, the great Pietist theologian August Hermann Francke, several of the latter's associates in Halle and London, and Halle-sponsored Lutheran ministers in the Danish colony of Tranquebar in India. The argument is that through networks of prolific correspondence and shared publications, the Anglo-American Reformed and German Lutheran/Pietist branches of the Reformation were drawn together in service of taking out the Protestant Christian Gospel message to Indigenous populations from North America to India, or, in the parlance of the times, from the West Indies to the East Indies. What emerged from this Boston–Halle–Tranquebar exchange were the theological and practical foundations for a refashioned "Protestant International" based on "a conservative but dogmatically minimalistic understanding of the Christian religion that combined an intensely Christocentric, biblicist, and experiential piety with an activist-missionary and eschatological orientation – a package which was now equated with being truly 'Protestant' or 'protestantisch,' respectively."[9] The nucleus in this story is a newly imagined Protestant Pietism, forged in the white heat of a vigorous anti-Catholicism during the War of the Spanish Succession and reinvigorated by the challenges of competing for souls among native

---

[8] Jan Stievermann, "A 'Syncretism of Piety': Imagining Global Protestantism in Early Eighteenth-Century Boston, Tranquebar, and Halle," *Church History*, 89:4 (2020), 829–56.

[9] Stievermann, "Syncretism of Piety," 829.

populations from the East to the West. The nodes were the Protestant centers of Halle Pietism, the English and Danish imperial capitals of London and Copenhagen, and gateways to new worlds of Gospel transmission from Boston to Tranquebar. What is important about this, apart from the story itself, is that it fundamentally changes how we think about global Protestant formation in the early modern period. It shifts attention away from traditional explanations based on later eighteenth-century Enlightenment ideas and helps us better understand the transatlantic awakenings of the eighteenth and nineteenth centuries which are still all too often understood in narrow geographical and denominational categories.

A more recent example of how religious networks can operate transnationally and even oceanically, this time across the Pacific not the Atlantic, is described in Helen Kim's book *Race for Revival: How Cold War South Korea Shaped the American Evangelical Empire*, in which she demonstrates that the rapid rise of evangelical voluntary societies in Korea in the era of the Cold War were not only parallel, but also deeply interconnected movements.[10] She shows that transpacific networks forged with South Korea were indispensable in refashioning American fundamentalism into mainstream evangelicalism. She follows the trails across the Pacific of three of the largest evangelical missionary non-profits, or "parachurches," which mark the re-emergence of American evangelicalism in the late twentieth century: World Vision, Campus Crusade for Christ, and the Billy Graham Evangelistic Association.

---

[10] Helen Kim, *Race for Revival: How Cold War South Korea Shaped the American Evangelical Empire* (New York, 2022).

Her story, like many others in the transnational spread of Christianity, begins with war. Through an unprecedented transpacific highway paved initially by the US military, American fundamentalists/evangelicals Bob Pierce, Bill Bright, and Billy Graham encountered South Korean Protestants Han Kyung-Chik, Joon Gon Kim, and Billy Jang Hwan Kim. The networks forged between these male religious elites on both sides of the Pacific, with help from fundamentalist and evangelical colleges in the United States (nodes where they met), became the foundation for the birth of World Vision, the internationalization of Campus Crusade, and the largest crusade ever hosted by the Billy Graham Evangelistic Association in Seoul, which remains probably the largest gathering of Christians at one time and on one site in history. With the Cold War as the backdrop, evangelical anti-communism as the engine, and religious networks as the mechanism, American evangelicalism gained new life though its Cold War imperial and racial projects in South Korea at the same time that South Koreans themselves activated their networks with Americans to expand evangelicalism for their own gain. They built their own religious empire, one that included, at times, collusion with an authoritarian South Korean regime and a Cold War American ally and empire. In the process, South Korean evangelicalism grew at an electric pace and has become one of the leading senders of evangelical missionaries in the twenty-first century. In this way, the junction boxes of Sun Belt evangelicalism and Cold and Hot War Korea reenergized American capitalistic and anti-communist evangelicalism and helped persuade it that the evangelization of the world was back on track, despite the closed doors of Soviet and Chinese state communism. Crucially, none of this was possible without preexisting military, educational, and ideological foundations, which religious networks built upon and exploited for their own advantage. What these two short examples, one transatlantic and the other transpacific, show is that transnational and transdenominational ways of thinking reveal important new dimensions to stories we mistakenly thought we understood.

Two other stimuli have influenced my approach to religious networks. The first is Niall Ferguson's recent book *The Square and the Tower: Networks and Power, From the Freemasons to Facebook*, which was turned into a television miniseries for Public Broadcasting Service called *Niall Ferguson's Networld*. Ferguson's book comes with a confessional preface in which he states that for too long he was casual in the way he thought about networks, preferring instead to write about hierarchies, states, and institutions, which collectively leave usable archives. His book "is an attempt to atone for those sins of omission" and, as befits such religious language, it starts with the network of printing presses that helped propagate the Lutheran Reformation beyond its origins with an obscure monk in an obscure German town.[11] Ferguson essentially brackets his history of networks between the revolution in print of the early sixteenth century and what he calls the second networked age characterized by the personal computer and the World Wide Web at the end of the twentieth century. As if appealing to the natural theology origins of the Gifford Lectures, Ferguson's chapter

---

[11] Niall Ferguson, *The Square and the Tower: Networks and Power, from the Freemasons to Facebook* (New York, 2018), xxv.

"Networks, Networks, Everywhere" finds ubiquitous networks in the natural world, from the human circulation system to colonies of ants, and from spiders' webs to beehives. With commentary that now seems eerily prophetic, Ferguson also refers to the speed with which an infectious disease spreads. Networks, both global and local, explain much of the patterns of disease transmission of the coronavirus pandemic from its hub in Wuhan in China through travel to Europe and then on to new hubs in New York, Boston, Houston, New Delhi, and the megacities of Latin America. Viruses and their evolving variants, like religious ideas, are transmitted from personal contacts that are themselves partly determined by the patterns of preexisting human interactions across borders, metaphorical and real. In addition, the speed of viral contagion and diffusion has increased exponentially in the contemporary world because of air travel, the rise of megacities, and the sheer number of active human networks.[12] Ferguson's conclusion is that, as with disease epidemics, "the network structure can be as important as the idea itself in determining the speed and extent of diffusion."[13] Moreover, key to the argument of this book is Ferguson's additional observation that networks intersect and interact with one another such that networks are important not only for the transmission of existing ideas, but also for the generation of new ideas and structures.[14] This is how virus variants have worked in the world of epidemiology: New variants evolve in new host populations and become

[12] Matthew O. Jackson, *The Human Network: How Your Social Position Determines Your Power, Beliefs, and Behaviors* (New York, 2019), 44–67.
[13] Ferguson, *The Square and the Tower*, 34.
[14] Ferguson, *The Square and the Tower*, 42.

more virulent and more transmissible. This is the point that David Martin was getting at in his reference to nuclei, nodes, and junction boxes, as places where new dynamic ideas and mechanisms are generated and transmitted along new routes. Following this line of thought, it is easy to understand why Ferguson begins his history of networks with the Lutheran Reformation, in which printing was crucial to its success. Cities with at least one printing press in 1500 were significantly more likely to turn Protestant, and printing-based networks worked far better for Protestants than Catholics during the Reformation era. Moreover, after the initial incursions into Roman Catholic control mechanisms were made, Protestants of all stripes, Lutheran, Reformed and Radical, became adept at establishing resilient network structures, first in northern Europe and then across the Atlantic.

Another network that plays a key role in Ferguson's analysis is freemasonry, which "furnished the Age of Reason with a powerful mythology, an international organizational structure and an elaborate ritual calculated to bind initiates together as metaphorical brothers."[15] Freemasonry expanded from the British Isles to continental Europe and the American colonies at around the same time as the rise of Methodism and was part of what Habermas has defined as an enhanced public sphere nourished in coffee houses and taverns and serviced by a rapid growth in print media, especially newspapers. David Hackett has recently shown how American freemasonry solidified what he calls an old-stock cultural Protestantism, but was flexible enough over time to

---

[15] Ferguson, *The Square and the Tower*, 111.

incorporate African Americans, Native Americans, Jews, and Catholics who bent freemasonry to their own cultural shape. In this way, networks can both reify the power of cultural elites and supply cultural outsiders with alternative networks based on similar rituals and practices.[16]

One of the weaknesses of Ferguson's approach is that networks are too often assumed to be operating separately from or in opposition to hierarchies, but that is not always the case. For example, the junction box that brought together European Pietists and British revivalists in London in the 1730s and 1740s possibly could not have happened, or at least would not have had the same impact, without the unlikely fact that the British monarchy was Hanoverian and the court was primarily German-speaking. Similarly, the Iberian networks of discoverers and conquerors that brought about the Spanish "conquest" of Mexico cannot be understood without the interaction with and domination by institutional hierarchies, especially the state-building ambitions of Ferdinand and Isabella and the Spanish Habsburgs. Conversely, the imperial policies of both British and Iberian hierarchies could not have reached as far as they did without mass printing or Catholic religious networks. In short, networks and hierarchies are rarely hermetically sealed from one another's influence. They are not opposition binaries.

As these examples show, it is appropriate at the outset to be clear about the strengths and weaknesses of using networks and nodes as analytical devices for investigating historical change in the history of Western Christianity

---

[16] David G. Hackett, *That Religion in which All Men Agree: Freemasonry in American Culture* (Berkeley, 2014), 1–16.

over half a millennium. Strengths include the ability to move beyond hierarchies, states, and denominations to look at more dynamic patterns of change across boundaries, borders, and oceans. Not only does this open up more fluid and mobile explanations of change, but, as we have seen, it also reveals a great deal about the underlying social and cultural contours that allow networks to thrive. Conversely, as Kate Davison has shown, network analysis can easily be based on anachronistic categories and may privilege progress and achievement, favor social scientific models, and depend upon bigger data sets which in turn prioritize the availability of such data in the Eurocentric world. Her conclusion is that network analysis is a valuable tool in a historian's toolkit, but it should not become an inflexible template.[17]

One potentially serious limitation of using networks to chart significant shifts in religious transmission in the early modern and modern world is that both the analytical categories and the sources privilege men over women. Men are mostly the entrepreneurs, soldiers, writers, organizers, and travelers. By contrast, most of the women who show up in the records traversing early modern networks are the exceptional women such as Marie de l'Incarnation, a baker's daughter from Tours in France who traveled both spiritually and geographically along seventeenth-century Jesuit networks to found the first Ursuline convent in North America. More or less contemporaneously, another group of nuns, this time originating in Spain, traveled halfway around the globe to establish the first female Franciscan convent in East Asia.

---

[17] Davison, "Early Modern Social Networks," 456–82.

This remarkable journey started in Toledo and ended up in Manila with stops in Cadiz, Guadeloupe, Veracruz, and Acapulco. Along the way, they stayed at inns run by women, female convents, and churches.[18] A century later, the freed slave Rebecca Protten retraced Moravian and slavery networks from the Caribbean Islands to eastern Germany and then on to West Africa, preaching, praying, and educating girls and young women along the way.[19] Although these women were obviously exceptional, they do show how religious networks opened up opportunities for extensive travel along arteries of migration and mission for women and men.

With those cautions in mind about the strengths and weaknesses of privileging religious networks, here is the content map for what follows. I will begin with a deeper theoretical analysis of what is at stake in this kind of history before looking at specific case studies. First, I will describe the printing and other networks that helped launch the Lutheran Reformation and then helped propagate Protestantism in early modern Europe. Paralleling that, I will look at a classic network created by the Catholic Counter-Reformation: the Jesuit Order. In particular, I will analyze how a nucleus was established and then follow the money as Jesuits established the first great network of schools and colleges in early modern Europe. Looking at how the Jesuits coped with almost half a century of suppression at the turn of the eighteenth century shows

---

[18] Sarah E. Owens, *Nuns Navigating the Spanish Empire* (Albuquerque, 2017).

[19] Jon Sensbach, *Rebecca's Revival: Creating Black Christianity in the Atlantic World* (Cambridge, MA, 2005). See also David Hempton, *The Church in the Long Eighteenth Century* (London, 2011), 82–86.

how networks build resilience and can survive unfavorable circumstances, even state repression. Moreover, the Jesuit crossings of state boundaries open up the historical complexities that network analysis can uncover.

For example, John T. McGreevy's recent book, *American Jesuits and the World*, tells the story of the transformation of American Jesuits from a feared, foreign religious order to a fundamentally American Catholic institution, which then participated in the imperial expansion of the United States at the end of the nineteenth century.[20] Reconstituted in 1816 as an order but under constant threat of expulsion from republican regimes, European Jesuits pushed out of Switzerland or Belgium and moved to the United States, becoming important players in religious contexts as diverse as Indian missions, urban ethnic parishes, and rural frontier settlements. Entering the American scene as refugees from republican European revolutions, their attitude to the American religious settlement was ambiguous. Although they considered state support for true religion to be a moral duty, they viewed church–state separation in America in a much more positive light, as there was little danger of an American expulsion of the Jesuits. Politically, along with the bulk of American Catholics, they tended to align with the Democrats, opposed abolitionism, and were anything but stout supporters of the Union cause.

---

[20] John T. McGreevy, *American Jesuits and the World: How an Embattled Religious Order Made Modern Catholicism Global* (Princeton, 2016). See also John T. McGreevy, *Catholicism: A Global History from the French Revolution to Pope Francis* (New York, 2022), which makes a serious attempt to understand Roman Catholicism as a global religious tradition.

Over time, the American Society of Jesus transitioned from an enterprise led by immigrant priests to one populated by Americans. These American Jesuits pursued a form of Catholicism that would be theologically orthodox but unashamedly American. Another symptom of this transition was the movement of America from a Jesuit mission field to a sending country. In the aftermath of the Spanish–American War, American Jesuits were called on for the first time to become foreign missionaries. In the somewhat awkward position of supporting a majority Protestant country in its conquest of an enfeebled Catholic empire, the American Jesuits were called on to replace the Spanish Jesuits in the Philippines. Employing their influence within the American imperial administration, Jesuits emphasized the importance of loyal American Catholics rather than meddling Protestant missionaries for the transformation of the Catholic Philippines in the American image. Starting as European refugees from persecution, American Jesuits evolved to become state allies in the rise of American imperialism.

As it turns out, even though McGreevy ends his story with the Jesuit encounter with American empire, he is interested in a longer and larger story. Considering his epilogue, McGreevy's story can be read teleologically as a prehistory to the American Jesuit influence on the Second Vatican Council, most importantly by John Courtney Murray. The history of the American Society of Jesus becomes a vital background for understanding the 180° turn in Catholic teaching from the Syllabus of Errors to *Dignitatis Humanae*. Committed to a Thomistic philosophy and prolific builders of a parallel system of Catholic institutions, they were increasingly favorably inclined towards the American ideal of religious freedom. By the twentieth century they were committed both to the American nation and to the global church, and American Jesuits helped to shape the face of postconciliar world Catholicism. McGreevy's story of a European Counter-Reformation religious society committed to a global evangelization project that hit the roadblocks of European political revolutions in the nineteenth century, then exported its missionaries to the United States, only to emerge as different kinds of players in twentieth-century global Christianity, is a rich example of how paying attention to transnational categories and the importance of religious networks reveals a great deal about the dynamics of religious change.

After considering the religious networks of the Reformation era and beyond, I will turn to the religious networks created by the growth of early modern empires, primarily Iberian and British. To what extent was a new version of Iberian Catholicism forged in New Spain and, using the work of William Taylor, what can be said about the *Theater of a Thousand Wonders* of shrines and images in New Spain?[21] Do physical objects of religious devotion reflect, create, and sustain a network? To what extent do the 500 or so shrines, which Taylor has called "a colonial archipelago of faith," operate as regional nodes in a network of images, pilgrimages, and circulating media of "cheap prints, novena booklets, and other devotional texts"?[22] Moreover, as this example shows,

---

[21] William B. Taylor, *Theater of a Thousand Wonders: A History of Miraculous Images and Shrines in New Spain* (New York, 2016).
[22] Taylor, *Theater of a Thousand Wonders*, 4.

networks can also flow in new directions as diasporic religion exported aspects of Latino Catholicism and devotion back to Catholic parishes in the United States and the Caribbean.[23]

Shrines are not the only material survival of religious devotion and community pointing to the significance of networks. Ann-Catherine Wilkening's investigation of the 2,600 gravestones (87 of which are of non-Europeans) in the Moravian settlement of Bethlehem, Pennsylvania, sheds new light on the demographic makeup of the early Moravian community. Far from being a monochrome settlement of German Pietist migrants, Bethlehem was a *Knotenpunkt* (junction or nodal point), bringing together people from five different continents. Bethlehem was not only the center of the early Moravian Western Atlantic world in the eighteenth century but was also constituted by many brethren of non-European descent, including Native Americans, Africans, and even some South Americans and Asians. In this way, a study of cemetery and burial records shows that early American Moravianism was a much more ethnically eclectic society than one might imagine from other more traditional written records of European Pietist migrations across the North Atlantic world.[24]

---

[23] Timothy Matovina, *Latino Catholicism: Transformation in America's Largest Church* (Princeton, 2012); Deborah E. Kantor, *Chicago Católica: Making Catholic Parishes Mexican* (Chicago, 2020); Thomas A. Tweed, *Our Lady of the Exile: Diasporic Religion at a Cuban Catholic Shrine in Miami* (New York, 1997); Elaine Peña, *Performing Piety: Making Space Sacred with the Virgin of Guadalupe* (Berkeley, 2011).

[24] Ann-Catherine Wilkening, "Beyond Missions and Memoirs: Tracing Non-European Brethren in Early Moravian Bethlehem," unpublished research paper, Harvard Divinity School (2019).

Still on the theme of networks of religious migration, next I will investigate the rise of Protestant missions and missionary societies across the Atlantic world from which they pushed out across North America, Latin America, Africa, and Asia. In one particularly important nodal point, Sierra Leone, a British imperial model for converting Africa to Christianity encountered a quite different kind of network of freed slaves who migrated from the American colonies up to Canada during the Revolutionary War, and then sailed back across the Atlantic to Sierra Leone. Out of this nodal intersection emerged a classic encounter between European elite missionary religion and populist Black spirituality, which had profound implications for the future of Christianity on the African continent. That will lead to a consideration of other nodal intersections, such as those between European Pietists and Anglo-American revivalists in the First Great Awakening and between white and Black forms of populist Christianity in Azusa Street and beyond which helped launch the most significant Christian movement of the twentieth century: Pentecostalism. I will then turn to an analysis of predominantly women's networks to ask whether they are fundamentally different from those constructed by men. I will finish with Ferguson's bookend of the digital revolution of the late twentieth century and offer a preliminary assessment of network Christianity and what it might mean for Christian belief and practice in the twenty-first century.[25]

---

[25] Brad Christerson and Richard Flory, *The Rise of Network Christianity: How Independent Leaders Are Changing the Religious Landscape* (New York, 2017).

There has often been a synergy between populist forms of evangelicalism and religious transmission through networks not controlled by established denominations and their hierarchies. In the epilogue of his book *The Democratization of American Christianity*, Nathan Hatch states that "Fundamentalism, the Holiness movement and Pentecostalism were grass-roots movements with democratic structure and spirit," which all began as networks of churches and leaders. "Fundamentalism emerged as a federation of co-belligerents opposed to centralizing ecclesiastical authority. Their institutional legacy was a loose network of independent churches, conferences, foreign mission agencies, Bible colleges, publishers, and radio stations."[26] In the absence of clearly defined hierarchies and institutional structures, these populist movements and their connections are often hard to trace, but there is no denying their ubiquity and dynamism in American and global Christianity or their capacity for throwing up controversial and demagogic leaders. They are often characterized by relatively unsophisticated theologies combined with highly sophisticated employment of networks of transmission media, including conferences, radio, television, and more recently social media and the internet, as the "network of networks."[27]

This pattern has continued into the contemporary period with a proliferation of networked churches, including Life Church, Acts 29, Blue Ocean Churches,

---

[26] Nathan Hatch, *The Democratization of American Christianity* (New Haven, 1989), 214.
[27] Heidi Campbell, *Exploring Religious Community Online: We Are One in the Network* (New York, 2005).

Harvest Network, and many arising out of a hegemonic megachurch. These networked churches have a variety of network connections, in person and online, a variety of theologies from explicitly Reformed to explicitly Pentecostal, and a variety of organizational and power structures. Depending on theological and personal factors, whoever creates and sustains the network determines whether it gives power to those without it, such as women and LGBTQ Christians, or consolidates power with those who already have it, mostly white men. When networks are used by people already in power, they often consolidate that power, but when used by people who lack power, as is the case with women, networks redistribute power more easily than in traditional denominations.

Within populist evangelical and Pentecostal faith communities, networks are also an integral dimension to mission strategy. Many American networks sometimes start or support networks in other countries as a form of mission, a way of fulfilling the Great Commission or asking the divine for a global "harvest." For example, the Acts 29 organization is a rapidly growing "global network of churches" engaged in extensive church planting in Canada, the United States, Latin America, Brazil, Europe, Africa, South Asia, and the Asia Pacific.[28] Harvest Network has international networks in Kenya, Haiti, Mexico, India, Thailand, and Ghana.

Although there are many networked churches birthed in the United States with extensions to other parts of the world, it is a mistake to assume that transmission is only in one direction. The story of the global outreach

---

[28] "Who We Are," Acts 29, www.acts29.com.

38

of American churches has been well told by American historians and sociologists, but the reverse story is less well documented.[29] With the global demographics of Christianity changing rapidly, greater understanding of the religious networks centered in other parts of the world, particularly sub-Saharan Africa, is going to be essential. For example, the Redeemed Christian Church of God (RCCG), with its network hub in Redemption Camp, Lagos, Nigeria, is a transnational network utilizing social media and considerable financial power to expand globally. The RCCG not only has the largest auditorium in the world, but also has built up an extensive network of churches in Nigeria, sub-Saharan Africa, Europe, the Caribbean, and the United States, including a new Redemption Camp in Dallas, Texas.

As these examples make clear, one of the intriguing dimensions to employing network analysis to global Christianity is the complex interactions between the local and the international. One obvious point, but one worth reiterating, is that one's selection of networks for study depends very much on one's social location – geographically, culturally, and according to broad faith traditions. For example, in the *International Religious Networks* identified by British and Scandinavian historians for the volume with that title, national traditions still played an enormous role in the choice of subjects and in the ascribed relative importance of their chosen networks.[30]

---

[29] See Robert Wuthnow, *Boundless Faith: The Global Outreach of American Churches* (Berkeley, 2009); Steve Brouwer, Paul Gifford, and Susan Rose, *Exporting the American Gospel: Global Christian Fundamentalism* (London, 1996).

[30] Gregory and McLeod (eds.), *International Religious Networks*.

Similarly, historians working on the early modern Iberian empires within the broad Catholic tradition work with a quite different set of sources and networks from those working on the British and Dutch empires within the broad Protestant traditions of Christianity. One of the challenges of this topic, therefore, is to acknowledge the limitations of social location and linguistic competence, including one's own, and to incorporate insights from a wide variety of transnational networks without losing focus on the benefits of network analysis.

Finally, it is wise to acknowledge that religion is far from the only sphere of human activity characterized by transnational networks of transmission. For example, the twentieth-century influence of the Bauhaus Movement, from persecuted centers in Germany to new nodes of influence in Paris and via Harvard to the United States, reflects a similar pattern of demographic mobility, ideological transmission, and use of visual media. A similar point could be made about the rise of jazz in New Orleans in the early twentieth century and its rapid expansion via Black migratory networks, facilitated by the rise of transmissible recordings. Moreover, Christianity is obviously not the only religious tradition to have central nodes and dispersed routes of transmission. Within Islam, the early Islamic pilgrimage routes across Saharan Africa to the Middle East and the importance of Singapore as a node of Sufi networks, Islamic literature, and oral histories across the Indian Oceanic world in the nineteenth and twentieth centuries are but two examples from historians in my own School of how scholars of other traditions encounter similar patterns of nuclei, nodes, and networks in the transnational circulation of people, ideas, and literature.

As I hope this chapter has made clear, interrogating the transmission of Christianity through networks, nodes (or junction boxes), and nuclei (classically the controlling genetic code of an organism) opens up exciting possibilities that are hard to realize from conventional emphases on denominational or national traditions alone. Consider this final example of transnational migrations of a religious tradition which shows even more clearly that what is at stake here is not just an awareness of geographical or spatial flows as a pedantic point of information, but that one cannot adequately understand the "lived religion" of any tradition's adherents without paying attention to their roots and routes of transmission.

The cultural anthropologist Todne Thomas has recently shown how a religious movement birthed in Britain and Ireland in the 1820s and 1830s, the Plymouth Brethren, was exported to the Caribbean Islands by Scottish Brethren missionaries. Members of these Afro-Caribbean Brethren communities subsequently migrated to the United States and set up religious congregations in the Greater Atlanta area. Thomas conducted a rigorous ethnographic study of two congregations, Dixon Bible Chapel and Corinthian Bible Chapel, the former with an Afro-Caribbean majority and African American minority and the latter with an African American majority and Afro-Caribbean minority. What she discovered is that these congregations forged deep ties of community, what she calls "kincraft," with recognizable DNA components from their complex Brethren and Africana origins, their middle passage journeys, Caribbean and American migrations, and their situatedness as Black evangelicals in the contemporary urban South.

This sophisticated tracing of roots and routes allows her to see dimensions of these Black religious traditions that do not yield easily to conventional ideas about the Black church, heteronormative family structures, and the social and political characteristics of Americans of African descent. She writes:

Influenced by diasporic consciousness and the anti- sectarianism and primitivism of Plymouth Brethrenism, church members understand their religious membership in transcendent, familial terms as an alternative to denominational boundaries. Church members construct a sense of belonging to broad kinship collectives (e.g., transnational diasporized family networks, family of God) through imaginaries that are not just distant and aspirational but also deeply meaningful and personal. Church members understand themselves to be part of trans-local networks of sister churches that are linked by their own migration histories.

According to Thomas, these Black evangelicals demonstrated a technology of kin-making, which brings together spiritual affinities as a family of God and the material concerns of mutually supportive sisters and brothers. This "spiritual kinship endures, even amid the mobilities and marginalizations of diaspora and race."[31] What is revealing about this ethnographic study of Black congregations created by the vagaries of mobile networks and unlikely nodes or junction boxes is that the "lived religion" of ordinary Black Christians is more vigorously brought to life in all its rich complexity than any explanation based on preconceived and reductive notions of the

---

[31] Todne Thomas, *Kincraft: The Making of Black Evangelical Sociality* (Durham and London, 2021), 199–211.

Black church, evangelical Christianity, and heteronormative constructions of families.

In Conclusion, I see six advantages to the theoretical
approach advocated in this chapter. First, it allows us
to cross boundaries, borders, and barriers to arrive at a
series of more mobile and flexible models of transmission. Second, it forces us to think more deeply about the
underlying social and cultural conditions supporting or
resisting such transmission. Third, it encourages us to
look more creatively at the crossroads or junction boxes
where religious personnel and ideas encounter different
traditions and from which something new and dynamic
can emerge. Fourth, it forces us to look more deeply at
the characteristics of the networks themselves and ask
more penetrating questions about what, in terms of personnel, ideas, and materials, is traveling along the networks. Fifth, it allows us to see that such traffic is not
always unidirectional, nor is it necessarily conditional
on the exercise of superior power, though inevitably any
sophisticated analysis of networks will reveal a great deal
about the structures of power underlying them. Finally,
it allows us to reconstruct religious communities with a
greater sense of fidelity to their inner and outer characteristics, and how they have evolved over time, than can
be delivered by more static analytical categories based on
nation states and singular religious traditions.

To give these conclusions a more theoretical turn,
they fit quite well into Sewell's "Theory of Structure,"
in which he suggests that both sociologists and social
historians often base their social analyses on *structures* of
power, resources, and relationships (like the girders of a
building), which "tend to assume a far too rigid causal

determinism in social life." "Structures," he concludes, "are not reified categories we can invoke to explain the inevitable shape of social life," but rather "call for a critical analysis of the dialectical interactions through which humans shape their history."[32] In this book I am suggesting that an over-concentration on conventional structures in the history of Christianity, whether hierarchical, national, denominational, or theological, has obscured the efficacy of human action and the dynamics of change, especially change from below and change that cannot easily be tracked through traditional sources. In that way, my highlighting of networks, nodes, and nuclei is not so much an attempt to create another analytical or theoretical structure as it is an attempt to show that the underlying dynamics of religious change are as constantly in flux as the evolutionary processes of nature itself with its DNA, genetic mutations, and environmental adaptations.

[32] William Hamilton Sewell, *Logics of History: Social Theory and Social Transformation* (Chicago, 2005), 151.

2

Religious Networks in the Reformation Era

~

Two networks transformed the early modern world. The first was the Iberian network of discoverers and conquerors that helped usher in an age of European world domination. The second was facilitated by a new technology, printing, which "helped to unleash the huge religious and political disruption we know as the Reformation, as well as to pave the way for the Scientific Revolution, the Enlightenment and much else that was antithetical to the Reformation's original intent."[1] The stakes could not be higher. What Ferguson calls "a religious virus that came to be known as Protestantism" disrupted an ancient ecclesiastical hierarchy, fractured into many pieces Europe's Catholic Christianity, and ushered in a long era of violent conflict that left few places unaffected.[2] Brad Gregory's *The Unintended Reformation* controversially takes the argument even further by suggesting that the Reformation disrupted Latin Christianity's integrated "worldview within which the overwhelming majority of Europeans lived and made sense of their lives."[3] Over the long run, so the argument goes, this integrated and relatively harmonious religious

[1] Niall Ferguson, *The Square and the Tower: Networks and Power, from the Freemasons to Facebook* (New York, 2018), 82.
[2] Ferguson, *The Square and the Tower*, 87.
[3] Brad S. Gregory, *The Unintended Reformation: How a Religious Revolution Secularized Society* (Cambridge, MA, 2012), 2.

45

worldview was unintentionally replaced by a fragmented civilization comprised of pluralism, capitalism, consumerism, and secularism.

This almost dispensational periodization both of a centuries-old integrated view of medieval society and of the impact of Protestant novelty underestimates the perpetual processes of negotiation between local reform efforts and re-establishment within the church, universities, and monasteries.[4] At least some of the rhetoric around medieval unity and integration was actually propaganda that arose in concert with rising stakes in the globalizing context of power struggles in the later fifteenth and early sixteenth centuries. The key question is not so much how new ideas disrupted a supposedly monochrome medieval consensus, but how reformed ideas interacted with other macroscopic changes to reshape the texture of European life on so many levels. Put another way, how then did an event of such huge and lasting consequence, which we call the Protestant Reformation, emerge from a small and unlikely event in a relatively unimportant town in Northeastern Germany in 1517? And how does the analytical framework of this book, namely networks, nodes, and nuclei, amplify our understanding of what happened and how it happened?

The nucleus in this story is Martin Luther himself and the revolutionary ideas he successfully propagated, especially the linked ideas of the freedom of the Christian and justification by faith alone. The nodes and the networks

[4] See Kathleen Davis, *Periodization and Sovereignty: How Ideas of Feudalism and Secularization Govern the Politics of Time* (Philadelphia, 2008).

are primarily the connections between Wittenberg and the other great centers of print publication and dissemination in Nuremberg, Augsburg, Basel, Strasbourg, and other cities in imperial Germany. Although print is what holds the story together and generates much of the narrative energy, it is important to state some caveats at the start which do not show up in Ferguson's more monochromatic analysis. The first is that the potential of print, including its emphasis on the Bible as the Word of God, had already been harnessed by Erasmian humanists for propagandist and educational purposes *before* the printing press helped the dissemination of Protestantism in Germany. Second, in many parts of Europe, and even in Germany itself, print often took a back seat to other forms of dissemination, principally through forms of oral transmission "via the personal networks created by mobile merchants, humanist scholars or itinerant students, through preaching campaigns or through the informal transfer of news and rumour prior to appearing in print."[5] Oral communication is not only crucial for a fuller understanding of how networks functioned in early modern Europe, especially given the low literacy rates, but also oral means of transmission inevitably changed the content of the communication.[6] What was spoken was not always the same as what was heard. In addition, Reformation ideas were promulgated by many other forms of network communication including hymns,

[5] Bob Scribner, Roy Porter and Mikuláš Teich (eds.), *The Reformation in National Context* (Cambridge, 1994), 219.

[6] For a nuanced analysis of how oral transmission could change the message, see Mark U. Edwards, Jr., *Printing, Propaganda, and Martin Luther* (Berkeley, 1994).

songs, woodcut illustrations, broadsheets, catechisms, and ditties and stories.

Even with those caveats in place, the sheer scale of print production and dissemination in Luther's Germany is quite remarkable, and Luther was unmistakably the center of it. In his fine account of how *Brand Luther* came to have such extensive influence, Andrew Pettegree begins with Luther himself, who emerged "as a writer of extraordinary power and fluency, a natural stylist in a genre that not to that point particularly valued these skills. In the process Luther created what was essentially a new form of theological writing: lucid, accessible, and above all short."[7] Luther, a little-known Augustinian friar in a minor university town, made his breakthrough into wider public consciousness with the publication of his *Sermon on Indulgences and Grace* which took on the medieval church's understanding of the sacrament of penance and indulgences. The sermon made quite a splash and was followed up by more vernacular pamphlets of a mostly devotional and pastoral nature. Meanwhile, an even more controversial Latinate story was brewing through Luther's public disputations and more subversive criticism of the papacy and clerical elites in which Luther's characteristic emphases on *sola scriptura* and the priesthood of all believers began to emerge more clearly. By the summer and winter of 1520, Luther's vernacular readers were aware that big controversial issues were at stake, and the conservative Catholic publicists who tried to refute Luther inexorably made the situation worse by making a point of it. Catholic opposition and censorship proved to be

---

[7] Andrew Pettegree, *Brand Luther* (London, 2016), xii.

ineffectual instruments of control, especially in cities and universities where emerging elites and ideas were hard to suppress.

As the controversy deepened, there were significant changes in the presentation and distribution of Lutheran propaganda that substantially increased the volume and impact of Luther's writings. The printing operation in Wittenberg was professionalized by Melchior Lotter Junior, and Lucas Cranach's woodcuts not only transformed the appearance and aesthetics of the Wittenberg publications but also helped transform the landscape of printing throughout Europe. In business parlance, Luther was now a brand leader and innovator, and he benefited from the increased competitiveness and lucrativeness of the printing industry. The more competitive the printing trade became in any given city, the more likely it was to turn Protestant. The bare figures are remarkable. Between 1517 and 1525 there was more than a forty-fold increase in the number of printed pamphlets, and by 1546 the "presses of the German-speaking land produced over six million vernacular treatises supporting or opposing the Reformation," one for every two people in the empire.[8] Luther's writings, 80 percent of which were in German, far exceeded those of anyone else.[9] According to Pettegree, over the course of the sixteenth century German printers produced more than 5,000 editions of Luther's works, and another 3,000 if one includes projects he was instrumental in propagating, including the hugely influential Luther Bible.

[8] Edwards, *Printing, Propaganda, and Martin Luther*, 172.
[9] Ferguson, *The Square and the Tower*, 83.

There is no question therefore that circulating print through a network of German printing presses in imperial cities, with Wittenberg as the unlikely center, played a crucial role in distributing the ideas and content of the early German Reformation. But if print was essential for *Brand Luther*, *Brand Luther* was also vital for the expansion of the German printing industry: "After Luther, print and public communication would never be the same again."[10] The economics of printing forced the creation of nexuses or printing centers because it was far cheaper to reprint works not protected by copyright than to ship large numbers of copies overland. Luther's own dominance of the press depended not so much on the number of his works as on the frequency of reprints. Hence, Luther's religious ideas helped urban elites reconceive and justify their economic practices, not only in the printing trades, but also in the wider economic order of towns and cities in the German empire.

Another important dimension to the dissemination of Lutheran ideas, bringing together print and oral culture, was the proliferation of hymnals and song sheets. According to one careful estimate there were more than two million hymnals, song sheets, and other hymn-related materials circulating in sixteenth-century Germany, and the overwhelming preponderance of all hymn printing was Lutheran.[11] The well-known printing centers of Nuremburg, Leipzig, Strasbourg, and Wittenberg accounted for more than half of the production, but

---

[10] Pettegree, *Brand Luther*, 338.
[11] Christopher Boyd Brown, *Singing the Gospel: Lutheran Hymns and the Success of the Reformation* (Cambridge, MA, 2005), 5.

hymn printing was also widely disseminated across almost fifty other German towns. Luther was himself a prolific composer of hymns and melodies, but the Lutheran laity, including women, also played an important part. Hymns were not only used in public expressions of Lutheran worship, but also in homes, workplaces, and other informal arenas. Hymns, as with later Methodist hymnody and Pentecostal songs, were effective ways of spreading Reformation theological ideas, both doctrinal and more practically pietistic, in accessible forms. The extent to which Lutheran theological ideas and confessional loyalties percolated down from elites to the broader population was largely owing to the successful distribution and singing of Lutheran hymns, especially in the homes of the laity. The format, size, structure, and content of Lutheran hymnals make clear that they were primarily printed not for the professional market, but rather for private lay use: "The Lutheran hymnal of the sixteenth century was foremost and most typically not a church book but a household book," and contributed more than other forms of Lutheran print to a devotional Reformation as well as a theological one.[12]

Understanding the importance of print to the Lutheran Reformation is a necessary but insufficient part of the explanation of how and why the Reformation gained strength in many different forms in many different national contexts. This takes us back to the previous chapter, in which it was stated that for religious networks to be successful, they need to be synergistically connected to other structural changes from which they benefit, but

[12] Brown, *Singing the Gospel*, 12 and 167–72.

do not create. As Bob Scribner noted many years ago, although there is no doubting the specific national characteristics of the Reformation as it took root in various places over time, it is also possible to identify some more-or-less consistent and generic themes. They included the preparatory and mediating role of continental humanism, the availability of a vernacular Bible, the importance of urban elites (especially the politically organized Estates), the corresponding weakness of the Reformation in traditional rural areas, and the overwhelming significance of the religious allegiances and policies of monarchs and rulers.[13] His conclusion was that for the Reformation to have an enduring existence anywhere, it had to become deeply embedded in national identities and contexts, so that, for example, for the sake of its durability and impact, the "Reformation in England" had to become distinctively the "English Reformation."[14] The same was true for most other countries.

So far, our treatment of Reformation networks has concentrated on print and the Lutheran Reformation, but within a generation Calvinism superseded Lutheranism as the most dynamic and widely disseminated form of Protestantism.[15] By the second half of the sixteenth

[13] Scribner, Porter, and Teich (eds.), *The Reformation in National Context*, 215–25.

[14] For a vigorous interpretation of the role of religion, vernacular literature, and a vernacular Bible in the creation of nationalism, see Adrian Hastings, *The Construction of Nationhood: Ethnicity, Religion and Nationalism* (Cambridge, 1997).

[15] Philip Benedict, *Christ's Churches Purely Reformed: A Social History of Calvinism* (New Haven, 2002), xv. This remains the most substantive treatment of the international spread of Reformed Protestantism. For a more thematic treatment organized around the issue of social

century Reformed Churches were firmly rooted in France, Scotland, England, the Netherlands, Hungary, and Poland–Lithuania. In the seventeenth century the colonizing efforts of the emerging Dutch and English empires carried Reformed Protestantism to North America and South Africa.[16] How did this happen? What were the nuclei, nodes, and networks of the early European reformed tradition? This story goes back to Huldrych Zwingli in Zurich and even more directly to his successor Heinrich Bullinger (1504–75), who built up an extensive network of correspondence and published many influential works. The most important of the early Reformed leaders was of course Bullinger's contemporary, John Calvin (1509–64). His monumental *Institutes of the Christian Religion*, first published in 1536, contains the nucleus of Reformed theology and his base in Geneva became the most important node of the international Reformed network. In both word and ecclesiastical practice, Calvin's theology was an intellectually compelling attempt to reconcile Christian freedom with godly order by way of the characteristic Calvinist emphases on divine sovereignty, providence, predestination, and church discipline. The last of these represents perhaps Calvin's "most famous legacy, for here was the blueprint – in its general structural outline – for the most widespread form of ecclesiastical order in the Protestant world." Calvin drew up a practical guide for the ordering of the church in Geneva,

order, see C. Scott Dixon, *Protestants: A History from Wittenberg to Pennsylvania* (Chichester, 2010).

[16] For a recent and superbly researched treatment of the transatlantic dimensions to the Reformed story, see David D. Hall, *The Puritans: A Transatlantic History* (Princeton, 2019).

which was spelt out in his *Ecclesiastical Ordinances* (1541). This prototype of the presbyterial–synodal system was not followed in exact detail throughout the Reformed world, but its underlying principles for the exercise of church governance and discipline marked out all the Reformed churches of the sixteenth century.[17]

Calvin's writings and Calvin's Geneva were the most important nuclei and node of the Reformed tradition, but they were not the only ones. Pierre Viret in Lausanne, Guillaume Farel in Neuchâtel, John à Lasco in Emden, and others within the Swiss Confederation and affiliated territories contributed to a growing Reformed "matrix" of scholars and preachers, churches and communities. This network was not without its heated disagreements and occasional ruptures, but it was held together by a broad allegiance to Reformed theological principles, the influence of hegemonic urban churches, periodic attempts to construct consensus as in the Second Helvetic Confession, and perhaps most important of all, by a vigorous anti-Catholicism that was much less tolerant of any accommodation to Catholic rituals than the Lutheran wing of the Reformation. The network was also sustained by a peripatetic band of Reformed scholars and preachers of no fixed abode, sheltering from the cold winds of persecution in their respective homelands, and by self-conscious attempts to grow the network, as in the more than 220 pastors dispatched mostly from Geneva to oversee the organization of worship in Piedmont and France in the decade after 1554.[18] By the

---

[17] Dixon, *Protestants*, 47–59.
[18] Benedict, *Christ's Churches Purely Reformed*, 119.

end of the sixteenth century the international Reformed network of churches, notwithstanding the intense dynastic and political pressures to which they were often subjected, displayed a remarkable fellowship and solidarity. "They shared personnel, eucharistic fellowship, and crucial elements of political outlook; they consulted with one another on issues of doctrine; and they offered one another their prayers and financial solidarity in time of need."[19] Examples include the *Harmony of Confessions* published in 1581, drawing together the articles of eleven different reformed confessions in response to the Lutheran Formula of Concord, and the collections raised for mutual support in times of affliction, as when the Duke of Savoy mounted a campaign to retake Geneva in 1589–93. But "plenty of raw human mobility also wove the disparate Reformed churches into a larger international community," for wherever one looks in the histories of the early Reformed tradition, the more examples there are of remarkable human travels along the arteries of the Reformed networks of churches, universities, and cities.[20] Jean Taffin was born in Tournai; trained for the ministry in Antwerp, Strasbourg, and Geneva; served churches in Aachen, Metz, then back to Antwerp; and later fetched up in Heidelberg, Haarlem, and Amsterdam.[21] The Reformed in Transylvania sent their aspirant clergy to study in France, Germany, England, and the Dutch Republic. Albert Szenczi Molnár studied at Wittenberg, Heidelberg, and Strasbourg, before spending time in the

---

[19] Benedict, *Christ's Churches Purely Reformed*, 291.
[20] Benedict, *Christ's Churches Purely Reformed*, 287.
[21] Benedict, *Christ's Churched Purely Reformed*, 288.

German universities of Herborn, Altdorf, and Marburg, while conducting an extensive correspondence with French and Flemish scholars.[22] John Knox spent twelve years of his life almost continuously on the move from Scotland to England, France, Geneva, Frankfurt, Dieppe, and back to Scotland.[23] Knox's career, according to Alec Ryrie, exemplifies in unusually stark terms the strengths and weaknesses of early reformed networks and perhaps of networks in general. "They can do some things superbly well: spread ideas, build contacts, shelter refugees, defend and rally those scattered and discouraged by persecution, support preachers, spread propaganda, establish orthodoxies, discipline dissenters in their ranks." What they and their human components could not easily do is engage in hard politics, make and effect diplomatic calculations, and effect change from above except in exceedingly rare cases when the network became integrated into, or coopted by, the instruments of power.[24]

The networks sustained by Protestants in the Reformation era consisted of overlapping connections based on print, correspondence circles, schools and universities, and refuges from overt opposition and persecution. Because they were based primarily on intellectual commitments and spiritual priorities, they could be sustained by ties of loyalty and solidarity even when the structures of hierarchies and power operated against them. The Reformed networks in France, Puritan migrations across

[22] Dixon, *Protestants*, 58.
[23] Alec Ryrie, "John Knox's International Network," in Jeremy Gregory and Hugh McLeod (eds.), *International Religious Networks*, Studies in Church History, Subsidia 14 (2012), 96–115.
[24] Ryrie, "John Knox's International Network," 115.

the Atlantic, and many other examples of Protestant survival in unfriendly local contexts show that networks could
survive and even thrive without official support.

This foray into the European Reformations through
the networks that helped the spread of innovative ideas,
what Torsten Hägerstrand has called "innovation diffusion as a spatial process," has concentrated on the Lutheran
and Reformed Reformations.[25] There were also myriads
of networks spawned by the more radical Reformation
traditions, such as the Anabaptists and their successors.
Indeed, networks probably played a greater role in the
trajectory of radical reformation groups because of their
lack of hierarchical sponsorship and their vulnerability to
persecution. For example, Martin Rothkegel has made a
compelling case that the Anabaptist Austerlitz Brethren
as early as 1528 constructed "a network of spiritually
united congregations" that functioned as a clandestine
international communion from Moravia in the east to
Alsace in the west. The node in this important story
is "the Holy Church of Austerlitz in Moravia," which
became the center of an Anabaptist denominational network called "The Fellows of the Covenant" under the
leadership of Pilgram Marpeck. Operating neither as an
ecclesiastical hierarchy as in the Roman Church nor as
a municipal or territorial based religious entity as in the
Lutheran and Reformed reformations, the Austerlitzers
pioneered a new form of a networked ecclesiastical structure, a "denominational network" that was "later paralleled by the rise of the Mennonites in the Netherlands

---

[25] Torsten Hägerstrand, *Innovation Diffusion as a Spatial Process* (Chicago, 1967).

and in the Low German territories, and from the seventeenth century onward by the British Baptist associations and the system of supralocal meetings of the Quakers." In short, this nascent denominational structure started as a survival and unifying network of radical persecuted Protestants and became one of the most influential organizing tropes in the history of Christendom. According to Rothkegel, "Marpeck and the network of Anabaptists he led played a key role in shaping an ecclesiological model based on voluntarism, which in subsequent centuries would make Christianity compatible with a modern pluralistic society."[26] Here is a case of ecclesial networks anticipating and benefiting from much wider structural changes in the early modern world.

This analysis of Protestant Reformation networks, Lutheran, Reformed, and Radical, stops short of the beginnings of the powerful networks of correspondence, print, and organizational innovations built by the Pietists, when improved literacy rates and female education added yet new dimensions. Potentially the largest and most radical network idea of all coming out of the Protestant Reformations was the deeply subversive doctrine of the priesthood of all believers. Nothing struck so deeply at the heart of the whole structure of the medieval Catholic Church than the notion of a general priesthood. But,

---

[26] Martin Rothkegel, "Pilgram Marpeck and the Fellows of the Covenant: The Short and Fragmentary History of the Rise and Decline of an Anabaptist Denominational Network," *The Mennonite Quarterly Review*, 85:2 (2011), 7–36. The quotations are taken from pages 27 and 8 respectively. See also Arnold C. Snyder, "In Search of the Swiss Brethren," *The Mennonite Quarterly Review*, 90:4 (2016), 421–551; Kat Hill, *Baptism, Brotherhood, and Belief in Reformation Germany: Anabaptism and Lutheranism, 1525–1585* (Oxford, 2015).

as Reg Ward has pointed out, it did not receive a full-scale theological treatment until Jakob Spener at the end of the seventeenth century, and the general history of Protestantism since then has been of a conscious evasion, even subversion, of this doctrine in favor of clerical establishments of one kind or another.[27]

At the same time as the Lutheran Reformation was roiling the Holy Roman Empire and John Calvin was producing his *Institutes of the Christian Religion*, one of the world's most powerful and enduring religious networks was arising within the very Catholic Church that the reformers were attacking. The Society of Jesus, founded by Ignatius of Loyola, arose out of a gathering of university students at the University of Paris in the 1530s and was given formal approval by Pope Paul III in 1540. It later emerged as the largest mission organization in the world. Although composed only of men, Jesuits were also spiritual directors of women and sometimes used women associates as catechists. Recent scholarship has paid attention to their immense investment in colleges and their cultural contributions to education, theatre, music, architecture, agriculture, and industry.[28] They expertly raised money, built libraries, educated Europe's Catholic elites, promoted civic engagement, pioneered scientific

---

[27] It is itself revealing how few serious historical treatments there are of the doctrine of the priesthood of all believers. A rare exception is W. R. Ward (ed.), "Pastoral Office and the General Priesthood in the Great Awakening," in W. R. Ward, *Faith and Faction* (London, 1993), 177–201.

[28] See John W. O'Malley, Gauvin Alexander Bailey, Steven J. Harris, and T. Frank Kennedy (eds.), *The Jesuits: Cultures, Sciences, and the Arts, 1540–1773* (Toronto, 1999) and *The Jesuits II: Cultures, Sciences, and the Arts, 1540–1773* (Toronto, 2006).

inquiry, constructed maps, employed the visual arts, and produced any number of grammars, vocabularies, catechisms, and confession manuals. Hence, they were not only enthusiastic missionaries, but also inexhaustible cultural dynamos. Although much depended on whether Jesuits entered foreign missions on the coattails of conquering armies or as missionaries to non-subjugated civilizations (black robes versus mandarin robes), they built a reputation for engaging foreign cultures not as domineering imperialists but as skillful adapters to local sensibilities.[29] But Jesuits also underwent a rigorous program of spiritual formation based on their founder's *Spiritual Exercises*, which helps explain not only their personal discipline, but also their enthusiasm for global mission. Markus Friedrich writes,

Even though this worldwide network of Europeans was and remained precarious … many Jesuits nonetheless tied the continents together through their lives and their experiences as wanderers between worlds. All this happened first and foremost in the name of the mission. That was the decisive purpose that brought the Jesuits overseas, inspired them to undertake their sundry ministries, and warranted the global network they created.[30]

In the methodological parlance of this book, the Ignatian *Spiritual Exercises* is where the nucleus of the Jesuit enterprise was located, and its increasingly global networks consisted of people, circulating letters and print, and, most visibly of all, colleges. They created what

[29] Andrew C. Ross, *A Vision Betrayed: The Jesuits in Japan and China, 1542–1742* (Maryknoll, NY, 1994).
[30] Markus Friedrich, *The Jesuits: A History* (Princeton, 2022), 574.

one historian has called "the biggest network of private schools Europe has known, with something in the order of five to six hundred distributed across the Continent."[31] My intention is to understand better how the *Spiritual Exercises* acted as the energy center of the Jesuit enterprise, then to look at the extensive network of the Jesuit educational system, especially how it was funded, and then to look at how the Jesuit networks fared during the suppression of the order at the end of the eighteenth century. Put simply, we will examine the Jesuit nucleus, follow the money that built the network, and compare the "virtual society" of the suppressed Jesuit Order with what came before and after.

Beginning with the nucleus, I want to examine further a connection that Michelle Molina has made between "the history of western subjectivity and the history of early modern global expansion," or, less technically, "how individual efforts at spiritual transformation had global significance."[32] In particular, Molina explores how "new thinking about self and world were key components of Jesuit evangelical efforts," and how Jesuit spirituality proceeded from self-reform to the reform of others. Central to her investigation is the comment by Arnold Davidson that "in trying to capture the different forms in which the care of the self has appeared, it is

---

[31] Olwen Hufton, "Every Tub on Its Own Bottom: Funding a Jesuit College in Early Modern Europe," in O'Malley et al. (eds.), *The Jesuits II*, 7.

[32] Michelle Molina, "A Heart-Shaped World: Jesuit Consolation Culture in a Globalizing World, 1500–1800," an unpublished paper delivered at Harvard Divinity School in spring 2008. I am very grateful to Dr. Molina for discussing her ideas with me.

essential to understand not only the ways in which the self became an object of concern, but also how one went beyond oneself, relating the self to something grander than itself."[33] With that in mind, she shows how the enormously influential Ignatian *Spiritual Exercises* were designed to reform one's self internally in the interest of a much greater cause, namely the conversion of the world's population. Beginning with introspective exercises of prayerful divine engagement and self-scrutiny, practitioners were encouraged to look outward to imagine the entire world.

Originally conceived as a month-long exercise in spiritual formation, the first "week" (not necessarily seven days) was devoted to "spiritual exercises to overcome oneself, and to order one's life." The second week was devoted to "the contemplation of the kingdom of Jesus Christ: the call of the temporal king as an aid toward contemplating the life of the eternal king." In these exercises the practitioner was encouraged to *imagine* the life of Jesus as he moved though synagogues and villages preaching the kingdom, and then to follow him. The practitioner was to ask for "an interior knowledge of Our Lord who became human for me, that I may love him more intensely and follow him more closely." Following meant bringing together the interior knowledge of Christ with an expansive vision of the redemption of the whole world. The practitioner was urged

---

[33] Arnold I. Davidson, "Ethics as Ascetics: Foucault, the History of Ethics, and Ancient Thought," in Jan Goldstein (ed.), *Foucault and the Writing of History* (Oxford, 1994). See also Mark R. Leary, *The Curse of the Self: Self Awareness, Egotism, and the Quality of Human Life* (New York, 2004).

to see the great extent of the circuit of the world, with peoples so many and so diverse ... I will see the various persons, some here, some there. First, those on the face of the earth, so diverse in dress and behavior: some white and others black, some in peace and others at war, some weeping and others laughing, some healthy and others sick, some being born and others dying, and so forth ... I will listen to what the persons on the face of the earth are saying; that is, how they speak with one another, swear and blaspheme, and so on. Likewise, I will hear what the Divine Persons are saying, that is, "Let us work the redemption of the human race."[34]

The third and fourth weeks were centered on Christ's passion and death and the resurrection appearances. Taken together, the four-part *Exercises* were a way and a means of bringing the divine into closer relation with sinful people and to prayerfully imagine a deeper discipleship.

Originally conceived as a thirty-day retreat, the Jesuits adapted and abridged the *Exercises* in various programs to suit the individual needs of the laity. What was new about this in the early modern period was not so much the religious content of the *Exercises*, which are well known to have had any number of medieval precedents, but that the audience, the laity, was being inviting into monastic spiritual disciplines. A combination of shortened *Exercises* to be completed in only eight days (or fewer) and the growth of retreat houses, where the *Exercises* could be directed, expanded the range of Jesuit spirituality to a much larger group of people, both religious and lay. Moreover, these

---

[34] George E. Ganss (ed.), *The Spiritual Exercises of Saint Ignatius* (Chicago, 1992), paragraphs 102–07.

disciplines occurred within a context of European imperial expansion and the growing circulation of the *Jesuit
Relations* (missionary reports) about what was happening
in different parts of the world.[35] In short, self-discipline
and spiritual formation, a key component of which was a
desire to see the rule of Christ over all nations, was a way
of universalizing the Christian message, and personal submission was a prelude to missionary action. Put another
way (using early modern language), in Jesuit spirituality
the religion of the heart was an expression of love for the
sacred heart of Jesus, and the sacred heart of Jesus was in
turn capable of embracing the entire world. In this way
the Jesuit nucleus, the Ignatian *Spiritual Exercises*, "was a
powerful tool of missionary spirituality that enabled individual practitioners to maintain self-discipline and focus,
even if deprived of a supportive community and familiar surroundings. The spiritual and intellectual preparation of the Jesuits made them ready to travel across
cultures, and capable of working alone even in hostile
circumstances."[36] There would have been no Jesuit
missionary network without Jesuit spiritual formation.[37]

The *Exercises* were essential to how the Jesuit Order
took shape, but they were also supplemented by the

[35] *Jesuit Relations* is the common abbreviation of *The Relation des Jésuites
de la Nouvelle France*, which were annual reports issued by the superior
of the Jesuit missions in New France to the Jesuit overseer in France
in the seventeenth century.

[36] Dana L. Robert, *Christian Mission: How Christianity Became a World
Religion* (Chichester, 2009).

[37] See Ananya Chakravarti, *The Empire of Apostles: Religion, Accommodatio,
and the Imagination of Empire in Early Modern Brazil and India* (New
Delhi, 2018); Bronwen McShea, *Apostles of Empire: The Jesuits and New
France* (Lincoln, NE, 2019).

Formula of the Institute, the short-form early rule of the order, and by the meticulously crafted *Constitutions*, which reflect the extraordinary organizational talents of Ignatius who turned the original charism and zeal of the *Exercises* into a well-organized global network. Within a generation, this network extended through virtually every country in Western Europe as well as Brazil, India, and Japan, and Ignatius himself traveled along the European routes of the network and even to Palestine. Somewhat unique to the Jesuits, by comparison with other Catholic orders, was their practice of mixing nationalities in any given mission, making the Jesuits "international in a way the other orders were not."[38]

One tension at the heart of the Jesuit enterprise directly parallels that between networks and hierarchies more generally: How could the networks of individual spiritual formation coexist with the ecclesiastically sanctioned pre-scriptions and proscriptions of the Catholic Church? Put another way, "the Jesuit tradition lives with the tension between a missionary commitment to life at the church's boundaries and an allegiance to the visible, hierarchical institution."[39] This tension could be, and was, a point of friction in the centuries ahead, but it was also a source of energy as the *Spiritual Exercises* became the foundation of the Jesuit Order's remarkable expansion to more than a thousand members before Ignatius's death in 1556.

If the *Exercises* supplied a flexible, disciplined, and relational spirituality for its devotees, the ubiquitous

---

[38] John W. O'Malley, "The Distinctiveness of the Society of Jesus," *Journal of Jesuit Studies*, 3:1 (2016), 1–16.

[39] Philip Endean, "The Spiritual Exercises," in Thomas Worcester (ed.), *The Cambridge Companion to the Jesuits* (Cambridge, 2008), 62.

network of colleges extended the Order's social and cultural influence in remarkable ways. But influence did not come cheap. In explaining how the Jesuits raised the money for their network of colleges without charging tuition, Olwen Hufton draws an analogy with modern fundraising by universities that raise money by cultivating elite and wealthy donors, borrowing and lending money, initiating building campaigns, and appealing equally to civic virtue and self-interest in attracting gifts and graduating talented students. Jesuits relied on a complex amalgam of funding, from popes and bishops to civic dignitaries and wealthy widows, but, as with fundraising for universities, the income stream was never guaranteed and there was never enough income to keep debt at bay. Jesuits soon discovered, as with university capital campaigns, that raising money for buildings was easier than paying for their upkeep, and although they mined every source of income, the default position for most of the pre-Revolutionary Jesuit colleges was one of hand-to-mouth indebtedness. Hufton's conclusion is that the whole Jesuit financial edifice, not unlike that of the rickety *ancien regime* financial system within which it was located, was by the end of the eighteenth century under the same kinds of stresses and strains that stoked wider revolutionary energies throughout the Atlantic world.[40] Debt or no debt, the Jesuit colleges, from the first foundation in Messina in 1548, through the opening of the influential Roman College in 1551, to the 120-plus colleges in Italy alone on the eve of the suppression of the Society in 1773, were a truly remarkable educational

[40] Hufton, "Every Tub on Its Own Bottom," 20.

achievement that contributed to the education of tens of thousands of students who in turn built their own networks of influence throughout Europe and beyond.[41] The financing and management of the network of Jesuit colleges required an immense amount of paperwork and bookkeeping, and the coordination of the studies in the Ignatian spirit demanded adherence to a common curriculum supplied by the *Ratio Studiorum*, written in 1598 and issued a year later. Moreover, the educational experiences of both boys and men equipped them for purposeful civic leadership in which piety and intellectual cultivation were designed to produce a sanctified society and a Christian civilization.[42]

The Jesuit schools and colleges also required and sustained an enormous intellectual and material investment in printed books throughout the whole spectrum of the *studia humanitatis*. The extent to which the Jesuits became cultural dynamos is illustrated, literally, by the publication and distribution of so-called "emblem books" in which spiritual and ethical truths were made memorable by pictures, maxims, and poems. According to O'Malley, the Jesuits produced more emblem books than any other group, publishing some 1,700 of them in the first half of the seventeenth century alone.[43] Ironically, the Jesuits exploited the new world of movable type and

---

[41] Paul V. Murphy, "Jesuit Rome and Italy," in Thomas Worcester (ed.), *Cambridge Companion to the Jesuits* (Cambridge), 71–87.

[42] Judi Loach, "Revolutionary Pedagogues? How Jesuits Used Education to Change Society," in O'Malley et al. (eds.), *The Jesuits II*, 78.

[43] O'Malley, "The Distinctiveness of the Jesuits," 10–12. See also John W. O'Malley (ed.), *Art, Controversy, and the Jesuits: The Imago Primi Saeculi, 1640* (Philadelphia, 2015).

book illustrations more assiduously than any other group since the early Lutheran reformers.

If the nucleus of the Jesuit enterprise was the *Spiritual Exercises* and the networks were primarily the colleges and their curricula, the two were brought together in the confraternities and sodalities organized for the college students. The confraternities had three primary characteristics: They inculcated Ignatian piety, they helped mobilize the laity in support of Jesuit missions and charity, and they drew members from all social classes.[44] They also extended the reach of Jesuit networks into local communities through charitable activities, catechizing, communion preparation, and fostering new vocations for the Order. The most important node of the Jesuit enterprise was Rome. It was there that Ignatius built the Jesuit organization and located the Superior General. Rome was also the location of the great foundational churches and the most important colleges, including the Roman College, later renamed the Gregorian University, and many European colleges, including the German and English Colleges, which in turn became sending institutions for the work of the Order throughout the continent and beyond. As Jesuit networks expanded geographically, they were knit together by a formidable epistolary network that sustained horizontal as well as vertical bonds within the order and diminished the spatial separation and loneliness of missionaries dispersed throughout the world.[45] The constant exchange of letters was at once an

---

[44] Murphy, "Jesuit Rome and Italy," 75–77.
[45] See Markus Friedrich, "Governance in the Society of Jesus: 1540–1773," *Studies in the Spirituality of Jesuits* (2009) 41, 1: 1–42.

administrative discipline, a connecting mechanism, and a religious practice in its own right.[46]

As beneficiaries of the imperial expansion of Western Europe in the early modern period, the sheer extent of the Jesuit reach into the non-European world is hard to overestimate. From New France and Latin America in the West to India, China, and Japan in the East, Jesuit missionaries encountered native peoples and ancient civilizations and relentlessly communicated and reported on their encounters. They built churches, missions, and colleges; disseminated and imbibed new knowledge; and were often sensitive intermediaries between European and non-European cultures and civilizations. But controversy and conflict were rarely far from the surface. From the Guarini reductions in Latin America to the Chinese Rites controversy, and from the Malabar Rites controversy in India to the Tokugawa persecutions in Japan, the Jesuits often found themselves at the center of irreconcilable conflicts between Christianity and other religious and civic traditions, and even within Catholic Christianity itself, as eighteenth-century popes sought to impose stricter standards of confessional orthodoxy on the outer edges of the Jesuit networks.[47] As the early modern papacy sought to impose more organizational and doctrinal control over an increasingly geographically diffuse church, Roman networks and Jesuit networks were sometimes at loggerheads with one another.

---

[46] See Paul Nelles, "Jesuit Letters," in Ines G. Zupanov (ed.), *The Oxford Handbook of the Jesuits* (New York, 2019), 44–72.

[47] See David Hempton, *The Church in the Long Eighteenth Century* (London, 2011), 57–82; Worcester (ed.), *The Jesuits*, 153–214.

Throughout the history of the Jesuits, controversy and conflict had frequently resulted in proscriptions and expulsions, but by the second half of the eighteenth century a more ominous storm tide was gathering against them. Once the heralds of the Counter-Reformation, by the mid eighteenth century, the Jesuit Order seemed to have become too powerful for its own good. From the Jesuit reductions in Paraguay to the bankruptcy of the Jesuits' mission in the French West Indies, and from the reforming energies of "enlightened" administrators in Portugal and Spain to a series of legal feuds in the Paris *parlement*, the Jesuits seemed to be on the receiving end of remorselessly bad news, all the more serious because it could neither be contained within a single country nor confined to a single cause. Beginning in Portugal with the expulsion of the Jesuits from the metropolitan mainland and the Asian and South American colonies in 1759, the dominoes of the demise of the Jesuit Order tumbled with inexorable rapidity. In 1764 the Society was dissolved in France; in 1767, following the infamous Hat and Cloak Riots of a year earlier, Charles III of Spain followed the Portuguese model by expelling the Jesuits from Spain and its colonies; Naples and Parma followed suit the same year; and in 1773 the most crushing blow of all came when Clement XIV, under irresistible pressure from the Bourbon powers, formally dissolved the society with the bull *Dominus ac Redemptor*. The papal dissolution naturally spelt the end of the Jesuits among the Catholic German states, within the domains of the Austrian Habsburgs, and in missions everywhere. It is tempting to attribute all this hostility to a primary cause, such as the impact of the Enlightenment or the influence of the

Jansenists, or to what Jonathan Wright has described as a "shared repertoire of supposed Jesuit abuse, ranging from regicide, to sexual perversion, to avaricious profiteering," but in truth the suppression seems to have been a combination of generic international unpopularity and discrete political events from country to country.[48]

Whereas in previous suppressions, Rome was generally a protected haven for the Jesuits, in 1773 they lost their spatial node. But what happened to the networks so energetically constructed over two centuries? Although we still lack an authoritative treatment of the Jesuits during the suppression from 1773 to their reconstitution in 1814, the outlines of the story are relatively clear.[49] There is no denying that the suppression dealt a serious blow to the entire Jesuit enterprise, as 23,000 Jesuits were thrust into potentially vulnerable positions, most of their properties were seized and their missions abandoned, their educational functions were passed on to other religious orders, and the Society's Superior General Lorenzo Ricci was incarcerated in Rome and never released. There were, of course, episodic stories of stoic endurance in many countries, such as Austria and Poland, but the two most notable sites of survival were ironically the Russian Empire and the United States. Under Catherine the Great's protection, the Jesuits in

---

[48] Jonathan Wright, "The Suppression and Restoration," in O'Malley et al. (eds.), *The Jesuits II*, 264. See also Friedrich, *The Jesuits*, 575–620.

[49] The published literature on the suppression period is relatively well known. I also want to acknowledge an unpublished research paper for my class by Victor M. Muñiz-Fraticelli, "Virtual Society: Jesuit Networks during the Suppression, 1773–1814," which stimulated many fresh ideas.

modern-day Belarus benefited from their scientific and educational prominence and thrived under less public and more private support from the papacy. In this one part of the world, the old Jesuit node in Rome and its epistolary and educational networks allowed the Jesuits to resume almost business as usual with a Vicar General, a workable hierarchy, and an educational network of colleges still committed to the Jesuit *Ratio Studiorum*, the durable blueprint of Jesuit education worldwide. Under the unlikely protection of successive Russian tsars and permission from the papacy, the Jesuits not only constructed a formal system of governance in the Russian Empire but also conferred affiliate status on Jesuits from many different European countries. Effectively, the Jesuits had a new and unexpected node. But it did not last. Ironically, the formal restoration of the Society in 1814 was quickly followed by its expulsion from major Russian cities in 1815 and from the Russian Empire in 1820. "An autocrat's whim could save the Jesuits, but it also could destroy them," is how one historian has described it.[50] A different pattern of survival emerged in the United States under the influence of John Carroll, Bishop of Maryland and an erstwhile Jesuit. American Jesuits benefited from an influx of Jesuits from the Russian provinces and from the emergence of Georgetown as the intellectual center of American Catholicism. In the United States the corporate structure of the Jesuit Order was virtually demolished, but

[50] Daniel L. Schlafly, Jr., "The Post-Suppression Society of Jesus in the United States and Russia: Two Unlikely Settings," in O'Malley et al. (eds.), *The Jesuits II*, 778.

its networked connections thrived in different forms. Outside Russia and the United States, Jesuits both suffered from suppression and benefited from the opening up of other cultural opportunities where they "played an active part in the centers of eighteenth-century enlightened sociality (academies, libraries, publishing houses, astronomical laboratories, scientific laboratories, and Masonic lodges)."[51]

During the four decades of suppression, the Jesuits were never eradicated by force, and they were able to maintain a skeleton of both formal institutions and informal networks that served them well when Pope Pius VII restored the Society of Jesus with the promulgation of *Sollicitudo Omnium Ecclesiarum* in 1814. There were about 600 remaining Jesuits when the Society was restored, and "by 1820 they numbered about 1,300; in 1850, 4,600; and in 1900, 15,073, when they had returned to almost all their former territories and were reaching out to new missions."[52] Whatever the bare numbers say, the Jesuit Order that was restored in 1814 was not the one that was suppressed in 1773, and the world order in which religious institutions had to operate had been seismically changed by the American and French Revolutions. But what the decades of suppression showed is that even without the support of political and ecclesiastical elites, and often their active hostility, the Jesuits were able to survive and, in some places, thrive by holding fast to their

---

[51] Niccolò Guasti, "The Age of Suppression: From the Expulsions to the Restoration of the Society of Jesus (1759–1820)," in Ines G. Zupanov (ed.), *The Oxford Handbook of the Jesuits* (New York, 2019), 918–49.
[52] Schlafly, "The Post-Suppression Society of Jesus in the United States and Russia," 772.

Spiritual Exercises, their educational philosophy, their habits of mind, and their informal and formal networks. They also kept meticulous archives, which allowed them to tell their own story and enable the rest of us to appreciate its importance.

What these studies of Reformation and Counter-Reformation era networks show is that in the sixteenth century, religious ideas intersected with other macroscopic changes in print and culture, commerce and social structure, education and civic engagement, and early modern globalization to produce changes of epochal importance. These changes do not easily yield their causes and consequences to analyses of singular religious traditions in particular nation states or geographical regions. Connecting the networks, identifying the nodes, and dissecting the nuclei at least allows for a wider range of analytical possibilities and helps guard against the Catholic and Protestant propagandized versions of religious history in the Reformation era which, over time, became associated with constructions of national identity.

Comparing and contrasting the Catholic and Protestant networks of the early modern period, Catholic religious orders, old and new, together with the rise of the Iberian empires, facilitated an earlier and more extensive global missionary impact than Protestant networks, which were more dependent on print, urban elites, universities, population migrations, and new kinds of ecclesiologies. The fact that early modern nation states had no real concept of religious toleration of minorities paradoxically helped religious networks thrive, even as they remained vulnerable to the dynastic feuds that the Reformation helped unlock. Religious networks, by their very nature, were influential instruments of change, but could never fully control the political and ecclesiastical conditions under which they operated. Ironically, the competitive energies unleashed by the Reformation and Counter-Reformation networks produced not only new venues of religious and political conflict, but also new means and methods of religious dissemination.

3

Religious Networks in the Age of Empire in New Spain and Africa

~

In the geographical spread and organizational construction of early modern European empires, "Religion functioned for Europeans as an organizing concept in the dynamics of conquest, enslavement, and revolution. They used religion to define the borders between peoples. And those boundaries influenced the shape and tenor of empires. Two religious boundaries warrant particular attention. The first is the border between Christians and non-Christians ... The second border is between Protestants and Catholics."[1] Unsurprisingly, therefore, two of the most striking developments in the modern history of global Christianity have been the respective strengths of Catholic Christianity in Central and Latin America and of Protestant and Pentecostal Christianity in mostly sub-Saharan Africa, both of which have roots in European colonialism. The aim of this chapter is first to shed light on these important stories by focusing on two early imperial case studies, one from the Iberian imperial conquest of New Spain and another from the British imperial project in West Africa, specifically Sierra Leone. Second, to what extent does the theoretical model of nuclei, nodes, and networks help us

---

[1] Katherine Carté, "Empires and the Boundaries of Religion," in Eliga Gould, Paul Mapp, and Carla Gardina Pestana (eds.), *The Cambridge History of America and the World* (Cambridge, 2022), Chapter 21.

understand better the various processes that produced such significant consequences for the global transmission of Christianity in the early modern and modern world.

First, then, I want to look at Catholicism and the Iberian Empire in New Spain. Recent scholarship on the history of colonial Latin America points to the centrality of religion to the whole colonial enterprise, but also pays close attention to "the variety and complexity of Amerindian societies before the Europeans' arrival," and to the reality that the dynamics of encounter produced a "new world" for "Africans and indigenous peoples as much as for Portuguese and Spaniards." Sensitive observers of this "new world," however much limited by the inevitable preponderance of elite colonial sources and archives, emphasize that religion should not be cordoned off from other aspects of life and is best analyzed neither as a "totalitarian and repressive force (principally a ready justification and vehicle for colonial domination) or as an essentially private or selfless activity (little more than the province of shaded cloisters, home altars and busy deacons)."[2] Rather, religion in colonial societies, as in the societies doing the colonizing, was pervasive, elusive, central to daily life and labor and legal processes, and to practices of control and resistance. My intention, therefore, is to analyze these dynamics, not primarily through the lenses of conquest and subjugation, which are quite well known, but rather to focus attention on various kinds

---

[2] For a helpful introduction to religion in colonial Latin America along with a carefully chosen selection of primary sources, see Kenneth Mills, William B. Taylor, and Sandra Lauderdale Graham (eds.), *Colonial Latin America: A Documentary History* (Lanham, MD, 2004). Quotations are taken from the introduction to the documents, xxi–xxxiii.

of networks, specifically around shrines and images, the pious devotion to Our Lady of Guadalupe, and diasporic Latin networks from Mexico back to the United States.

Alas, I have to begin this third chapter with a historian's confession. Based on superficial reading and the ignorance that often besets us English-speaking scholars, I had hoped to present a persuasive interpretation of how my focus on networks, nodes, and nuclei would fit very neatly into the encounters between Iberian empire builders, with their accompanying friars and priests, and native peoples in New Spain. Already mapped out in my mind was a narrative that went something like this. Territorial conquest and demographic subjugation in New Spain were quickly followed by a Catholicization that featured an interconnected network of shrines and sacred places within which there was a clearly delineated hierarchy of places, images, and cults, all serviced by the circulation of ubiquitous devotional materials, in both visual and print forms. Crucial to my explanation was the existence of well-traveled pilgrimage and processional routes, the blood arteries of religious penetration. Of vital importance to my constructed narrative was the existence of clearly identifiable centers and peripheries, both in terms of geographical space and in terms of shrines and objects of devotion. In this dendritic networked system, I expected to show that the nuclei would be specific geographic locations, such as Mexico City and Tepeyac, and singularly specific devotions such as to Our Lady of Guadalupe. Vital to my project was the ability to show that long-distance pilgrimages from peripheries to centers, similar to those in European Catholicism, were what sustained the networks.

Alas, so much of what I assumed to be the case turned out not to be so. My first instinct was to squeeze the evidence for the last piece of juice to support my theory; my second was to give up and pick another topic. But there is a third and more creative way.

In his important study of the five hundred or so colonial shrines to miraculous images of New Spain, *Theater of a Thousand Wonders*, William Taylor concludes:

> shrines by definition reached beyond the local, but the history of image shrines in New Spain is less about a few central places interlocking with secondary shrines than it is about hundreds of clusters of communities with more parochial loyalties and sacred landscapes, where one devotion seldom eclipsed all others …Where the webs of communication and circulation for regional shrine images can be traced, they show more movement of things and information about celebrated images and shrines than of people traveling to and from them.[3]

In other words, this is not primarily a network/web of pilgrimage routes or of well-orchestrated colonial or ecclesiastical propaganda, but rather a loose federation of sensuous devotional sites dedicated to images and apparitions of the Virgin Mary, Christ and the Cross, and the saints of the church. Their integrative power lay not in their proven connectivity of people, things, and places, but in their ubiquitous appeal to the most visually compelling, devotion inspiring, and emotionally enchanting

---

[3] William Taylor, *Theater of a Thousand Wonders: A History of Miraculous Images and Shrines in New Spain* (New York, 2016), 554–55. I am grateful to Professor Taylor for conversations and advice beyond the printed page without which this section could not have been written. All interpretive errors are, of course, mine alone.

images and sacred personnel of the Catholic Church. Some regional shrines had pre-colonial associations, most did not; some were located in important colonial cities and centers of population, but many were not; some were established within the first half a century of the conquest, but most were founded in the long seventeenth century; some connected with themes and motifs from Iberian Catholicism, but there were also substantial differences, including the number of dark Christs and green crosses. Above all, shrines were sacred places where divine presence, power, and miraculous intervention met human desires for aesthetic beauty, transcendence, and healing. Taylor's book suggests that the shrines were regarded as little heavens on earth, ports in a storm, storehouses of wonder, genealogical deposits of forebearers' devotion, and sites for sensory exuberance and ritualistic expressions of dance, poetry, and music. They were affectionately cared for and sanctified by age and the loving marks of decades of touch and wear.[4]

Of all the images and shrines rooted in New Spain, but capable of transnational extension to other parts of the world, the emergence and growth of devotion to Our Lady of Guadalupe stands out as the most significant. In an important essay on "Places of Our Lady of Guadalupe in Eighteenth-Century Mexico," William Taylor concludes:

As the fame of Our Lady of Guadalupe reached into remote corners of the future Mexico, the image was on the way to becoming a dominant symbol. But it was a peculiar kind of dominant symbol, one that tended to reinforce the importance of many localities and images more than ordering a vast

---

[4] Taylor, *Theater of a Thousand Wonders*, 551–65.

spiritual geography. Territories of recognition and devotion were much larger than territories of sacred travel; as important as alms collectors, missionaries, pastoral visitors, and other official carriers may have been to the territorial reach of particular images and shrines, much of the dissemination occurred in secondary ways from provincial places and unofficial sources rather than from the main shrine.[5]

The point is that the widespread distribution of paintings and cheap reproductions of Our Lady of Guadalupe within Mexico and among people of Latin American descent everywhere "were likely to take on lives of their own rather than propel the viewer to Tepeyac."[6] That is largely the case now, even when mass transit has opened up the possibility and reality of long-distance pilgrimage, and was even more true of the colonial period when "pious wayfarers sought less for individual salvation in far-away places than for divine presence and favor in the landscape of home."[7] In terms of the overarching themes of our study, what is being described here is a different kind of network from, say, the printing presses of Luther's Germany or the dependent schools and colleges of Ignatius of Loyola's Rome, though neither print nor the Jesuits are entirely absent from this story either.

---

[5] William Taylor, *Shrines and Miraculous Images: Religious Life in Mexico Before the Reforma* (Albuquerque, 2010), 137–38.

[6] Taylor, *Shrines and Miraculous Images*, 137–38. In an example of periphery to center network transmissions, in the seventeenth and eighteenth centuries, a surprising number of fine paintings of the American Guadalupe found their way back to Spain – to convents, churches, and wealthy households. I owe this suggestion to William Taylor.

[7] Taylor, *Shrines and Miraculous Images*, 137–38.

To understand the historical evolution of this different kind of network, it is advantageous to know something about the origins and growth of the devotion to Our Lady of Guadalupe, from its supposed beginnings at Tepeyac in the early sixteenth century to its hagiographical promotion by the "four gospels" of the mid seventeenth century, and from the establishment of its annual feast-day celebrations in the 1690s to its vigorous efflorescence after Pope Benedict XIV's papal bull of 1754. Over time, the Virgin of Guadalupe became the most popular and geographically expansive of the many Marian shrines and images in colonial and postcolonial Mexico, but the point is that the devotional power of the image transcended its geographical and temporal specificities and did not depend on establishing Tepeyac as the center of a dominant tradition of pilgrimage.[8] In this way, the image of Our Lady of Guadalupe was able both to transcend the various political and dynastic shifts of power in Mexico's struggles for independence and to serve a nationalizing purpose without quite becoming "the temple of the national religion."[9] Guadalupan devotion in the colonial period was centered more on provincial shrines and pilgrimages than on a national pilgrimage network focused on Tepeyac, and in the postcolonial period, Guadalupan devotion was carried by Mexican migrants to other parts of North America and far beyond. Primacy among the

---

[8] For an authoritative recent discussion of how, when, and where the devotion to Our Lady of Guadalupe emerged and grew during the colonial period, see Taylor, "Mexico's Virgin of Guadalupe in the Seventeenth Century: Hagiography and Beyond," in *Shrines and Miraculous Images*, 97–115.

[9] Taylor, *Shrines and Miraculous Images*, 145.

sites of this devotional diaspora is the second Tepeyac, a sanctioned replica of the Mexican site located in Des Plaines, Illinois. Replete with a digital copy of the original image from Tepeyac and imposing sculptures of the Virgin and Juan Diego, this is the world's second most-visited Guadalupan shrine and maintains close contacts with the primary site in Tepeyac.

In a powerful study of the "devotional capital" that sustains these shrines and others, Elaine Peña has shown how Guadalupan shrines in central Mexico and the Chicago area are "transnationally linked by doctrine, tradition, aesthetic/physical replication, and early-twentieth-century labor circuits." The shrines are at the center of festivals, pilgrimages, daily rituals of cleaning and maintenance, and devotional piety which participant observation can identify, but not fully absorb. Peña's account of being on pilgrimage with a group of other women to Tepeyac evokes the earthy complexity of motivations and the rich variety of holy pieties: "Love and respect for La Virgencita outweigh all other motives. But pride, money, family ties, the quest for freedom, curiosity, devotional capital, and the need for guidance, protection and forgiveness mold the experience. Each peregrina's motivation for walking is distinct."[10]

What kind of a network, then, is the devotion to the Our Lady of Guadalupe, and what are its nodes and nuclei? In part, it can be explained in the conventional terms of flows of personnel, images, and information, first in colonial Mexico and then to other parts of the

[10] Elaine A. Peña, *Performing Piety: Making Sacred Space with the Virgin of Guadalupe* (Berkeley, 2011), 57.

world. It has at its center, its nucleus, a powerful image, a compelling foundational myth, and an inspiring narrative; it reflects and negotiates colonial conquest, religious authority, and indigenous and ethnic solidarity; it both reinforces local loyalties and transcends national boundaries; it has a unified core of doctrines, aesthetics and devotions, but it attracts "devotional capital" from many different experiences and motivations; it is not repudiated by religious authorities, most of the time, but sometimes creates problems of control for ecclesiastical institutions; above all, it powerfully unites Latin American Catholics and their diasporan communities in a loose but sensuously evocative federation of faith and culture.

Beginning in the early twentieth century, the Virgin of Guadalupe and other Mexican inspired devotions to the Blessed Virgin Mary, the infant Jesus, and saints traveled the migrant labor networks of Latino Catholics from El Paso to Chicago. Once the parish citadels of nineteenth-century European Catholic migrants from Ireland, Italy, Poland, and Eastern Europe, more than one-third of the parishes in the Archdiocese of Chicago now have Spanish language masses serving a remarkably diverse mix of national groups and generations of migrants. Mexicans began arriving in Chicago in large numbers in the 1920s, often as a result of incremental migration networks chasing changes in production and labor supply. In an evocative study of *Chicago Católico*, Deborah Kanter shows how Chicago's traditional Catholic parishes became Mexican through the work of religious orders such as the male Claretians and the female Cordi Marians, the cultivation of distinctive forms of Mexican piety and the virtual takeover of strategic parishes such as

Our Lady of Guadalupe in South Chicago and St Francis of Assisi in the Near West Side. These parishes became important centers of immigrant assimilation, sacramental devotion (baptisms and funeral masses), ubiquitous votive candles, ethnic youth organizations, and beloved images of the Sacred Heart of Jesus, the Virgin of San Juan de los Lagos, Our Lady of Guadalupe, and a host of other saints connecting Mexican provinces and Chicago's Catholic parishes. Up and down the generational and spatial networks of migration, Mexican Americans constructed a popular and lively Catholic culture that fused their Mexican and Catholic identities. Crucial to that formation were the various ways in which the image of the Virgin of Guadalupe was at the center of parish churches (often after colorful processions from Mexican sites), feast days, and other popular devotions. For example, in St Pius V Church the painter Edward O'Brien painted "The Mother of the Americas" depicting Our Lady of Guadalupe "entering a tableau of Mexican history from the conquest to the expressways of Chicago. Juan Diego gazes at the Virgin on one side, while the members of a Mexican American family, rosaries in their hands, likewise contemplate her image."[11] This is one of many instances of Guadalupan images in Pilsen parishes processed from Mexico or created in situ. While predominantly Mexican parishes have come and gone with the labor and immigration cycles, the images are durable connections between devotional landscapes in Mexico and Chicago. In this way, "real presence" is able to move with migrants and pilgrims

---

[11] Deborah E. Kanter, *Chicago Católico: Making Catholic Parishes Mexican* (Urbana, 2020), 112.

and the material objects not only travel along networks but are constitutive components of the networks themselves.[12]

How, then, can one explain the durability and transnational transmission of Guadalupan piety over almost half a millennium, and what is at stake for its devotees, past and present? Robert Orsi has proposed that in our study of religion "we let the gods out of their assigned places and that we approach history and religion through a matrix of presence." He states that a dominant characteristic of modern historiography is to treat Marian devotion of all kinds as "representations of social or psychological facts, symbols of something else, but nothing in themselves." Describing this as "modernity's ontological singular," he states that "interpretations share the assumption that what is happening when the transcendent breaks into time is not what appears to be happening to the men and women to whom it is happening, nor is it what they say has happened to them."[13] To frame our understanding of Guadalupan piety this way is not to deny the realities of structures of power or cultural embeddedness, or to be forced into a post-enlightenment discourse on miracles or divine intervention; rather, it is to treat presence seriously both for the images and artefacts of devotion and for those expressing devotion.

As with presence, so with place. In a fine parallel study of *Our Lady of the Exile: Diasporic Religion at a Cuban Catholic Shrine in Miami*, Thomas Tweed works his way to a theory of diasporic religion privileging place: "mapping, meeting and migration because all three are involved as

[12] Jimmy O'Leary, "The Virgin Materially Constructed," unpublished research paper, Harvard Divinity School (2019).
[13] Robert A. Orsi, *History and Presence* (Cambridge, MA, 2016), 59, 251.

groups draw on religion to make their own space and find their own place."[14] As the pious make their own spaces, the spaces also make them. He sees the diasporic religion of Cuban Catholics in Miami as neither primarily locative nor supralocative, but translocative (moving symbolically between the homeland and the new land) and transtemporal (moving practitioners between a constructed past and an imagined future). It is a mistake to think that all diasporic religions, even those with a shared devotion to the Virgin, share exactly the same functions in exile, but those who retain a close attachment to a homeland shrine and an ancient Marian devotion carry with them the exilic themes of presence, place, and performance.

Bringing the story up to the present, each year more than twenty million pilgrims travel to the Virgin of Guadalupe's shrine at Tepeyac. One distinctive devotional practice captured in photographs and analyzed by Jennifer Scheper Hughes is the carrying of replicas, images, and portable shrines on the backs of the pilgrims. In this devotional labor, pilgrims turn their bodies into mobile altars and they "carry replicas to the shrine so that they can visit and draw power from the original. When the pilgrim arrives at the devotional matrix, in this case at the Basilica, the power of the replica is reactivated and renewed so that, returning home to its place of origin, it preserves and maintains its potency in local and domestic devotion."[15] While this is

[14] Thomas A. Tweed, *Our Lady of the Exile: Diasporic Religion at a Cuban Catholic Shrine in Miami* (New York, 1997), 136–42.
[15] Jennifer Scheper Hughes, "God-bearers on Pilgrimage to Tepeyac: A Scholar of Religion Encounters the Material Dimensions of Marian Devotion in Mexico," *Religion and the Arts*, 18:1–2 (2014), 156–83.

the case for pilgrims within Mexico itself, it also holds for distant pilgrimages, from Chicago and elsewhere, who value not just the image of the Virgin but also its actual physical empowerment derived from a journey to the foundational shrine in Tepeyac. Intriguingly, the practice of carrying replicas on the backs of the pilgrims is not only a "fusion of European Christian iconography with indigenous Mexican conceptions of religious materiality, but also reflects a pre-conquest practice of 'god-bearing' in Mesoamerican religious practices."[16] In this way, ubiquitous devotion to the Virgin carries both pre-colonial and post-colonial resonances for the devoted.

As material constructions of the Virgin Mary travel along the networks of ethnic and national diasporas, whether Polish, Czech, Italian, Cuban, or Mexican, they assist in the formation, reformation, and reinforcement of the networks they travel, and they help establish new nodes of exilic Catholicism closely adapted to the particular cultural traditions they represent.[17]

What, then, is the balance sheet of treating the shrines and images of New Spain and Cuba, and their subsequent transnational exports, as part of our story of networks, nodes, and nuclei? Clearly, these five hundred or

[16] Hughes, "God-bearers," VII. Conclusions.
[17] For good examples of how this works for different traditions, see Robert Orsi, *The Madonna of 115th Street: Faith and Community in Italian Harlem, 1880–1950* (New Haven, 2002); Joseph Sciorra, *Built with Faith: Italian American Imagination and Catholic Material Culture in New York City* (Chicago, 2015); Jill M. Krebs, *Our Lady of Emmitsburg, Visionary Culture, and Catholic Identity: Seeing and Believing* (Lanham, MD, 2016); Deirdre Cornell, *American Madonna: Crossing Borders with the Virgin Mary* (Maryknoll, NY, 2010).

so shrines in New Spain with an additional cast of millions of mass-produced or homemade likenesses of their matrix images moving along migration trails and into the homes, villages, and neighborhoods of the devoted do not constitute a formal and carefully designed network with a clearly demonstrated purpose. This is more a network of devotion based on shared images and symbols located in specific places but capable of translocal expansion. They were sometimes promoted by ecclesiastical elites and sometimes repressed when they teetered over the edge into the realm of unacceptable populist expressions, but mostly they were regulated, tolerated, and even celebrated. They were often sponsored and supported by other networks, such as those operated by the Franciscans and the Jesuits (in print and pastoralia), and they had to be developed and maintained. This not only gave new opportunities for popular devotion, but they also served as recipients of fundraising networks around almsgiving, print selling, and image production. Above all, they were places where the immaterial divine could be encountered through material representation of the virgin, the crucified Christ and the historic saints offering hope and protection against the dangers and vicissitudes of daily life. Places where the divine could be embraced and evil resisted.

My second story of networks within the context of empire relates to the British Empire, evangelical Protestantism, slavery abolition, and the Christianization of Africa. In this case the nucleus is the threes "Cs" of Christianity, commerce, and civilization, as predominantly evangelical Protestants across the Atlantic world envisioned a world in which slavery could be eradicated and the African continent could be transformed by the civilizational values of colonial elites.[18] In this story, the most important nodes are London, Nova Scotia, and Sierra Leone, and the networks are vigorously transatlantic. In an important recent book on evangelicals and British public life, Gareth Atkins employs the insights of Actor–Network Theory developed by Bruno Latour and others to trace evangelical "networks that spanned the Church, universities, armed forces and imperial officialdom, and which connected London and the regions with Europe and the world."[19] According to Atkins, "this was a ramifying web of pious individuals, tied together by shared beliefs, to be sure, but cemented by social contact and intermarriage and lubricated – or perhaps driven – by patronage and ambition."[20] Interstitially located between the Hanoverian world of deference and patronage and the Victorian world of subscription-based voluntary philanthropic societies, the evangelical "Fathers of the Victorians" carved out a remarkable power base that extended into the two ancient universities, Oxford and Cambridge, the Church of England's parochial structure, the boards of the Bank of England and the East India Company, and some of the most important

---

[18] See Leslie T. Shyllon, *Two Centuries of Christianity in an African Province of Freedom: Sierra Leone, A Case Study of European Influence and Culture in Church Development* (Freetown, Sierra Leone, 2008); Maya Jasanoff, *Liberty's Exiles: American Loyalists in the Revolutionary World* (New York, 2011); and James W. St. G. Walker, *The Black Loyalists: The Search for a Promised Land in Nova Scotia and Sierra Leone, 1783–1870* (Toronto, 1993).

[19] Gareth Atkins, *Converting Britannia: Evangelicals and British Public Life, 1770–1840* (Woodbridge, 2019), 2.

[20] Atkins, *Converting Britannia*, 3.

government agencies tasked with supervising Britain's imperial expansion. These networks were more extensive and more influential than the well-known Clapham Sect and offer support to the view that "evangelicalism in the eighteenth century was inherently a connection-making creed."[21] As their ubiquitous correspondence and diaries show, these fin-de-siècle evangelicals were aided in their religious civilizing mission by the well-established patronage and clientage networks of Hanoverian Britain and by the national surge of popular evangelicalism sponsored by the Methodists and Dissenters who were mostly excluded from the centers of power but were willing allies in Britain's national and international godly mission.

Central to that godly mission in the decades after the loss of the American colonies was a powerful combination of antislavery mobilization, missionary zeal, commercial ambition, and civilizational hubris. The first and most important node where these forces came to be operational, the blueprint for the global Christian empire envisaged by the evangelicals, was Sierra Leone in West Africa. This was the location of attempts by British evangelical antislavery activists to set up a model settlement for freed slaves in Africa, whence they had been so violently captured. The first such planned settlement of freed slaves in Africa was conducted under evangelical auspices and ended in disaster. The so-called "Province of Freedom," which was initiated by the formidable antislavery activist, Granville Sharp, in 1787 for freed British slaves, was a grim failure, wracked by disease, desertion,

---

[21] Atkins, *Converting Britannia*, 8.

and disillusionment.[22] Within a year of arrival, more than half of the almost four hundred settlers had died, run away, or been discharged.

But the second attempt five years later was both more unusual and more promising and depended for its success on another network created by the vicissitudes of empire, this time in the American colonies and Canada.[23] In 1792 Thomas Clarkson's brother, John, was dispatched to Nova Scotia to recruit Black empire loyalists to make the journey back across the Atlantic and settle in Sierra Leone. In Clarkson's almost millenarian words, this was no less than an attempt to "civilize and Christianize a great Continent, to bring it out of Darkness, and to abolish the Trade in Men."[24] Most of the eleven hundred men and women of African descent who migrated from Nova Scotia to Freetown in 1792 were once North American slaves. The Black Nova Scotian community from which this reverse transatlantic migration originated had its roots in the promises made to Black enslaved people in the American colonies by the British in return for their assistance in the American Revolutionary War. Some of these unlikely empire loyalists brought with them a religious faith birthed in colonial revivals that was given a further

[22] The story is well told by Lamin Sanneh, *Abolitionists Abroad: American Blacks and the Making of Modern West Africa* (Cambridge, MA, 1999), 41–43.

[23] For the American context of the Sierra Leone story and other attempts to create settlements of freed slaves in West Africa, see Ryan J. Butler, "Transatlantic Discontinuity? The Clapham Sect's Influence in the United States," *Church History*, 88:3 (2019), 672–95; Eric Burin, *Slavery and the Peculiar Solution: A History of the American Colonization Society* (Gainesville, 2005).

[24] Quoted in Atkins, *Converting Britannia*, 155.

evangelical twist by the red-hot evangelicalism preached by Baptists and Methodists in Nova Scotia.[25] They were also imbued with some of the spirit of democratic republicanism that fueled the American Revolution and which was to lead to uneasy relations with their colonial evangelical sponsors who saw themselves in a life-and-death struggle against the radical ideas of the contemporary French Revolution. Here was a migrating network of onetime slaves forged out of imperial failure and revived by the transatlantic spread of populist evangelicalism.

Out of this unlikely community of migrants came David George, born a slave in Virginia in 1743 and revived in South Carolina before the American Revolution, who then became the first Black Baptist pastor in Canada and the first Baptist pastor in Africa. He left a spiritual autobiography that was transcribed from oral delivery and published in the *Baptist Annual Register* (1790–93). According to this narrative, George, while still a slave, picked up the various Christian influences that wafted around the southern colonies in the 1760s and 1770s. White Anglican plantation religion, the influence of slave believers, and New Light Baptist preaching all played their part in bringing him eventually to a classic evangelical conversion experience of awareness of sin, self-loathing, and joyful release. This was not quite a classical conversion narrative, however, for George was illiterate at the time of his conversion. Only later did he extract from the biblical narratives the formal template for his own experience. "I can now

---

[25] For the distinctive flavor of this evangelicalism as preached by the likes of Henry Alline, William Black, and Freeborn Garrettson, see George A. Rawlyk, *The Canada Fire: Radical Evangelicalism in British North America 1775–1812* (Kingston and Montreal, 1994).

read the Bible," he states later, "so that what I have in my heart, I can see again in the Scriptures," indicating that "the oral and the personal was anterior to the written and the discursive element in his experience."[26] Here, then, is an example of how a European tradition of penitential Christianity and release from sin could be stripped of its literary superstructure and act directly in the experience of a Black enslaved person who experienced both a real physical bondage and a perceived spiritual bondage.

George's conversion was followed by his British-assisted migration north to Nova Scotia during the American Revolutionary War. The Black inhabitants of Nova Scotia were already a people in motion before a surprisingly high percentage of them decided to make the voyage across the Atlantic in the opposite direction from their enslaved ancestors. Just as West African enslaved people were a captive people in motion along well-established slave-trade networks long before they arrived at the slave ports of the Bight of Biafra, the Nova Scotians had a migration history before they departed from Halifax for Sierra Leone. The dislocations of the American Revolution had resulted in the migration of substantial numbers of free Black people to the cities of Savannah, Charleston, and New York. Scholars have shown how religious practices that were diversely spread across the southern plantations coalesced in more significant ways in the Eastern

---

[26] Bruce Hindmarsh, *The Evangelical Conversion Narrative Spiritual Autobiography in Early Modern England* (New York, 2005), 321. See also the account in Rawlyk, *The Canada Fire*, pp. 33–43. For a modern edition of George's spiritual autobiography, see Grant Gordon, *From Slavery to Freedom: The Life of David George, Pioneer Black Baptist Minister* (Hansport, Nova Scotia, 1992).

Seaboard cities during the Revolution. Partly benefiting from client–patron relationships with the British military, partly facilitated by the greater population density of the cities, and partly fueled by a new generation of Black preachers, small but fast-growing Black churches emerged from the chaos of war and mobility. David George, George Liele (1750–1820), Andrew Bryan (1737–1812), Jesse Peter, and Brother Amos all helped preach and pastor new churches among Black populations in Silver Bluff, Savannah, the Caribbean Islands, and eventually Nova Scotia. One scholar concludes that "religious transformations such as George's planted among former slaves who had just become nominally free British subjects the means to engage and define their liberty across a wider terrain, an expanse once the exclusive spiritual and political domain of their masters."[27]

Just as a popular form of Black Christianity emerged from the migration of free Black people to Eastern Seaboard cities during the war, their subsequent migration northwards to Nova Scotia aided the process of new religious formation. Populations forced together to experience new freedoms on the move found solace, opportunity, and community support networks within emerging Black churches. Nova Scotia added yet another dimension, because it was already being "revived" by transplanted revival preachers from the British Isles and North America. David George and a growing number of Black migrants from the southern colonies added to the mix. In a sense, Nova Scotia emerged as an ethnic

---

[27] Alexander X. Byrd, *Captives and Voyagers: Black Migrants across the Eighteenth-Century British Atlantic World* (Baton Rouge, 2008), 166.

and religious junction box not unlike the Azusa Street community that played such a significant role in the launching of Pentecostalism in the early twentieth century. George and other Black preachers virtually had a captive audience of Black refugees. George's combination of American revivalist and Nova Scotian New Light evangelicalism was first preached to the Black empire loyalists in Canada and was then carried back to Sierra Leone, where it encountered an even more diverse cultural melting pot.[28]

The Sierra Leone Company that was launched in 1792 to fund and organize the model settlement was a genuinely commercial venture with shares and subscriptions, but it never delivered on its own lofty expectations. The Act abolishing British participation in the slave trade (1807) was quickly followed by the Sierra Leone Transfer Bill, which brought the whole project more squarely under the control of the colonial government and led to African recaptives from all over the continent being settled there.[29] British colonial administrators envisaged the colony being Christianized and civilized (the words were often interchangeable) through the creation of model villages supervised by ministers and schoolteachers and united by the universal application of rules and sacraments. This tidy reapplication of the European Christendom model of the territorial ecclesiastical parish as the chief engine of Christianization lacked many of the elements that made it work, after a fashion, in Europe.

---

[28] Rawlyk, *The Canada Fire*, 33–43.
[29] For an excellent survey of the complicated political and commercial forces at work in this transition, see Atkins, *Converting Britannia*, 143–67.

In Sierra Leone there were no resident squires supplying a measure of economic stability and social deference, no fully agreed Christian tradition and authority to impart (there were instead representatives from a proliferation of European missionary societies and religious traditions, and no resident bishops), and little homogeneity among the idealized settlements. These parish-style villages, quaintly named after British people, places, and battles, "transformed Freetown into a Black diaspora, a bustling entrepôt of refugees at large, with Freetown becoming a creolized, Caribbean-style cultural experience on African soil, a teeming crossroad of African and Western ideas stirred with an admixture of religious elements, Muslim, Christian and indigenous."[30] So extravagant was the diversity that the CMS German missionary linguist Sigismund Koelle in his *Polyglotta Africana* (1854) was able to document some 120 different languages spoken in the colony.

What is particularly significant is the way in which the Freetown Nova Scotian contingent operated simultaneously both as missionaries and as the objects of mission. At the same time as they were being disciplined into model Christian settlements, they were Christianizing, albeit African American Christianizing, the African recaptives. Here are multiple levels of engagement that give rise to some revealing encounters. The British organizers of the Sierra Leone colony reported in 1795 that the Nova Scotians in their religious observances were punctual, sabbatarian, well-dressed, and disciplined, but

---

[30] Lamin Sanneh, *Disciples of All Nations: Pillars of World Christianity* (Oxford, 2008), 127–28.

that some had imbibed "very inadequate or enthusiastic notions of Christianity; a few perhaps who set up hypocritical pretensions to it."[31] Part of what was happening in Freetown was a version of the contest between European establishmentarian Christianity and new forms of populist evangelicalism, primarily Methodist and Baptist, that was being played out in many different geographical locations in the British Isles and North America, but the demographic collisions and cultural resonances of Sierra Leone also produced distinctively African expressions. The historical trail of what was going on stemmed in one direction from the eighteenth-century Great Awakening, and in another from the African American missionary impulse, but there were also strands of European pietism, with its radical distrust of religious establishments, and slave religion, with its heart-stirring aspiration for spiritual and physical liberty.

What came out of these different strands were not only competing visions of how Christianity should function in new colonial spaces, but also different constructions of the kinds of Christian selves that should be fashioned. Consider, for example, the following three encounters.

The first is between the evangelical Anglican governor of Sierra Leone from 1793 to 1799, Zachary Macaulay (1768–1838) and David George. Macaulay, the English gentleman, regarded George and the Nova Scotians he represented as antinomians, a most "seductive" creed in which there were "No means to be used, no exertions

---

[31] *An Account of the Colony of Sierra Leone*, 2nd ed. (1795), 80, quoted by A. F. Walls, "A Christian Experiment: The Early Sierra Leone Colony," *Studies in Church History* 6, G. J. Cuming (ed.), *The Mission of the Church and the Propagation of the Faith* (Cambridge, 1970), 107–29.

to be made, no lusts to be crucified, no self-denial to be practiced." Instead, they constructed their faith round instantaneous conversions, "inexplicable mental impressions and bodily feelings," and the "delusive internal feelings of a corrupt imagination." After a twelve-hour discussion and debate between the two men, Macaulay's observation was that if any Nova Scotian believers were asked how they knew themselves to be children of God, they would answer not from proof drawn from the Bible "but because (perhaps) twenty years ago I saw a certain sight or heard certain words or passed thro a certain train of impressions varying from solicitude to deep concern and terror and despair thence again thro fluctuations of fear and hope to peace and joy and assured confidence."[32] Macaulay believed that God's evangelical kingdom in Africa could not be built from such ephemeral and transient materials.

A similar conclusion was reached by one of his successors as governor, Sir Charles MacCarthy (1764–1824), an Anglican from a Roman Catholic background, and "an establishment man, and a soldier, with a very clear idea of where his duty lies, and an acceptance of the alliance of religion and duty." MacCarthy was certainly no evangelical, and his vision of Christianization and civilization in Africa was to divide the Sierra Leone colony and then the entire continent into ecclesiastical parishes within which universal baptism would make a uniform Christendom.[33] Not even the European missionaries

---

[32] Rawlyk, *The Canada Fire*, 37–41.
[33] A. F. Walls, "A Colonial Concordat: Two Views of Christianity and Civilization," in Derek Baker (ed.), *Church, Society and Politics* (Oxford, 1975), 293–302.

with their evangelical roots could buy into that vision, never mind the Nova Scotians, and never mind the even more eclectic recaptives. W. A. B. Johnson (1787–1823), a CMS missionary, told MacCarthy that he would not baptize more Africans

unless God first baptized their hearts. He [MacCarthy] said that the reason so many were baptized on the Day of Pentecost was that the Apostles despised none. I replied that they were pricked in the heart, and that I was willing to baptize all that were thus pricked in the heart. He thought baptism an act of civilization, and that it was our duty to make them all Christians.[34]

Here are two visions of how Africa should be Christianized: One is territorial, liturgical, and universal, a product of the Anglican (or Catholic) civilization that constructed it; the other is providential, experiential, and emotional, a product of a very different set of experiences.

Our third encounter is probably the most significant of all. Moses Wilkinson, a blind, disabled slave from Virginia, escaped to Nova Scotia during the American Revolution and was one of those who sailed to Freetown in 1792. As someone who had suffered more than most from the perfidy and broken promises of white officials and who practiced and preached a populist evangelical message (he gave out his hymns and texts from memory), Wilkinson objected to the official Christianity of the Sierra Leone colony. One suspicious colonial official who showed up to mock his preaching came away impressed by his ability to affect his hearers He wrote:

---

[34] See W. Jowett, *A Memoir of the Rev. W. A. B. Johnson* (London, 1852), 94, quoted by Walls, 'Two Views of Christianity and Civilization,' 300–1.

Many of the wise and learned in this world, if they were to see and hear such a man as our brother, professedly engaging in endeavouring to lead their fellow creatures from sin to holiness, would at once conclude it to be impossible for them to effect the object which they have in view. Experience, however, flatly contradicts such a conclusion. Numbers have been led by their means to change their lives.[35]

Colonial officials were justifiably nervous about the enthusiasm, antinomianism, indiscipline, and potential political radicalism of Black preachers like Wilkinson, but there was no denying the fact that their version of Christianity was the one most likely to succeed among the burgeoning communities of recaptives deposited by the British Navy in Freetown. A shared suffering of body and spirit, and a shared sense of being marginalized by the structures of economic and political power, enabled preachers like Wilkinson to build a base of communal authority that could not be matched by colonial officials or white missionaries.

To these quite different visions of how freed Africans and transplanted African Americans should reconstruct their selves, their communities, and their continent can be added still more layers of interpretation carrying enormous consequences for the globalization and indigenization of Christianity. Working out of the Sierra Leone experience, the religious independency and charismatic authority exemplified by the Nova Scotians and recaptive converts have been described as threshold phenomena that can thrive "at the boundary between establishment values and the ideals of a people in transition."

[35] Sanneh, *Disciples of All Nations*, 173.

In other words, Christianity does not have to be regarded as a mere extension of Western norms but carries within it "pre-thematic local resonance" for those on the frontiers of "disruption, dislocation, resettlement, and restoration."[36] In short, Christianity does not have to come encased in centuries of European civilization even when colonial administrators are ostensibly in charge.

We should not underestimate the energy and achievements of both Wesleyan Methodist and Church Missionary Society missionaries and others in building schools, colleges, churches, and parochial discipline in Freetown and the surrounding villages in Sierra Leone, but over the long run the realities of colonialism set their own limits.[37] For the kind of Christianity forged by ex-African slaves in South Carolina, Nova Scotia, and Sierra Leone to thrive beyond local boundaries required the practical defeat of the European Christendom model, a vernacular Bible (translation as empowerment), and the transmission of Christianity shorn of Western cultural specificities and receptive to Indigenous religious sensibilities.[38] In Sierra Leone, for example, receptive Yoruba diviners who were "thoroughly at home in the world of divination, visions, and the crowded company of unseen spirits, welcomed the challenge of missionaries saying they were happy to add

[36] Sanneh, *Disciples of All Nations*, 176.
[37] See Bronwell Everill, *Abolition and Empire in Sierra Leone and Liberia* (Basingstoke, 2013).
[38] For more sustained and far more expert analyses of how these processes operated, see Andrew F. Walls, *The Missionary Movement in Christian History: Studies in the Transmission of Faith* (Maryknoll, NY, 1996) and Andrew F. Walls, *The Cross-Cultural Process in Christian History* (Maryknoll, NY, 2002).

the Christian divinity to the Yoruba pantheon because a place already existed for that."[39] What Sanneh has called "the local religious grammar" of rites, customs, and language shaped the emergence of a distinctively African form of Christianity and laid the foundations for its mass transcontinental appeal in the nineteenth and twentieth centuries.[40]

It is difficult to overestimate the importance of this process for the remarkable expansion of Christianity in Africa in the modern period. Eventually, however, there was to be no happy ending in Sierra Leone, for the Christianity that was minted by the combined and often contradictory efforts of missionaries, settlers, recaptives, and colonial officials has been largely obliterated by the political anarchy and civil war of recent times. Nevertheless, something very significant happened at the turn of the eighteenth and nineteenth centuries in colonial West Africa. Apparently inconsequential selves, refashioned in and out of slavery by the unlikely resources of populist evangelical Christianity, demonstrated a capacity for large-scale transformation not just in North America but also in the continent from which they had been so brutally seized and so serendipitously resettled.

David George's unlikely narrative and faith journey need to be located within the context of the networks built around the transatlantic slave trade, colonial warfare, population migrations, popular pietism and evangelicalism, the rise of empire, the colonization of Africa, the growth of the Protestant missionary societies, and

---

[39] Walls, "A Christian Experiment," 128.
[40] Sanneh, *Abolitionists Abroad*, 125.

the geography of the slave trade. Although his life is singular and unique, its trajectory resonates with some of the most powerful forces of his time. His is one of the more powerful examples of the exodus stories so beloved by Black Christians, and of the rise of African Christianity in both North America and Africa, which has reshaped the trajectory of global Christianity from the nineteenth to the twenty-first centuries. Given the projections from the Pew Foundation surveys about the growth of sub-Saharan African Christianity up to 2050 and beyond, this story about the evangelical and later Pentecostal surge of Black Christianity is one of the most significant in the entire history of Christian transmission over two millennia.[41] It could not have happened without the networks and junction boxes we have been discussing.

Networks and nodes also have their limitations. Paralleling the Sierra Leone experiment was a distinctively American version of African colonization in the neighboring territory of Liberia. Fronted mostly by the American Colonization Society from 1822 to 1847, and united by little other than an attempt to settle free African Americans in West Africa, the Liberian colonial experiment could never transcend the growing sectional tensions in the United States over slavery and could never quite decide whether it was a model agrarian prototype for Africa, a missionary republic entrusted with the conversion of Africa, or both. Unrealistic expectations, inadequate funding, divisions

---

[41] Pew Research Center, *The Future of World Religions: Population Growth Projections, 2010–2050* (April 2, 2015).

among its supporters, disturbing on-the-ground moral controversies, and uninspiring leadership all contributed to the clouding of the American millennial vision to convert Africa. The missionaries who began to flow in from the various denominational societies in the 1830s found themselves struggling to make an impact even on the American settlers, never mind the recaptives or Indigenous peoples. "Liberia," according to Tom Whittaker, "was unique in being the colony of a voluntary society," and was never an imperial project of the American government, as evidenced by the lack of state naval support by comparison with Sierra Leone.[42] It nevertheless became the focal point for very many voluntary networks comprising America's benevolent and missionary empires, but it also illustrated the strengths and weaknesses of those networks. The colonial republic of Liberia never became the node for the Christianization of Africa, or, for that matter, for the resolution of America's trials and tribulations over slavery and race control.

As these forays into religion and empire in the Americas and Africa make clear, Christianity, through

---

[42] Tom Whittaker, unpublished chapter for a forthcoming Harvard University PhD thesis entitled "The Missionary Republic: American Evangelicals and the Quest for a Christian Nation, 1787–1837." I am grateful to him for many stimulating conversations and ideas that have improved this chapter. For Liberia, see also Marie Tyler-McGraw, *An African Republic: Black and White Virginians in the Making of Liberia* (Chapel Hill, 2007). For wider issues around race and empire from different perspectives, see Brandon Mills, *The World Colonization Made: The Racial Geography of Early American Empire* (Philadelphia, 2020); Sylvester A. Johnson, *African American Religions, 1500–2000: Colonialism, Democracy and Freedom* (New York, 2015).

its collaborative and subversive alliances with imperial power, whether Catholic and Iberian or Protestant and Anglo-American, has the capacity to deliver popular cultures of devotion of extraordinary power, durability, and transmissibility, and also to perpetrate cultural rape and cruelty of unimaginable proportions. No evaluation of the balance sheet, however uneven it may be, can rest on the ideologies and actions of hierarchical elites alone, but has to consider networks and nodes, some of which are surprising and hidden from view.

What this chapter has sought to demonstrate is that, however useful religion was to the early modern imperial projects of Britain and Spain, and however much they relied upon the same Christianizing tools that had been forged over centuries of European civilization, unanticipated nuclei of popular devotion, new and unplanned nodal sites of transmission, and informal networks, both elite and popular, produced new forms of Christian devotion and new routes of transmission. One of the most controversial and keenly debated topics in religious historiography is the extent to which newly emergent traditions of Christian devotion in colonial sites were simply reapplications of old established and exploitative control mechanisms or were themselves forged and owned by once colonized populations.[43] Concentration on colonial elites and institutional history mostly advance the former interpretation, concentration on informal networks and native agency advance the latter. Both stories need to be told, but the more transnational

---

[43] For an informed recent discussion of these themes, see Johnson, *African American Religions.*

the locations, the more non-denominational the focus, and the more openness there is to treat seriously the unauthorized devotional complexity of popular religiosity, the more important it is to uncover the informal transmission mechanisms of religious networks and their unlikely junction boxes.

4

The Protestant International

Pietism, Premillennialism, and Pentecostalism

~

The aim of this chapter is to apply our general organizing principle and method – nuclei, nodes, and networks – to some of the most significant developments in the English-speaking Protestant world in the past four centuries, including the transition from pietism to evangelicalism, the explosive growth of Protestant missions, the origins of premillennial dispensationalism and its contribution to the rise of fundamentalism, and finally the worldwide spread of Pentecostalism. None of these developments can be studied within a single denominational or national tradition and none can be understood without coming to terms with their nucleus of ideas/theologies, the nodal points of their transmission and dissemination, and the transnational networks that facilitated their growth. I am grouping these world-changing developments under the general heading of the Protestant International, the rise of which:

was intimately connected with an evangelical revival centred in the Atlantic world, which promoted and benefited from an expansion in print culture, the movement of peoples and the rise of civil society. The revival was initially not so much international as transnational, or oblivious to national boundaries ... For Protestants, then, the international message grew in symbiosis with the technologies required to broadcast and receive it. The result was an informal spiritual empire, a network of formal bodies that federated believers across increasingly distinct national boundaries.[1]

The Protestant International was far from static or monochrome. It was demographically mobile, denominationally diverse, and prone to inner conflict and fragmentation. I wish to make clear at the outset that there are other possible ways of constructing the Protestant International, such as that presented by Kathleen Carté in her recent book on "Imperial" Protestantism, which states, "Before the American Revolution divided it, an interlocking system of religious networks, societies, and communities connected distant protestants to one another across the British Empire."[2] Important though those networks were, my attention is less on networks attached to institutions and governments – institutional history, if you like – and more on the populist energies of what she calls "awakened protestants," whose stories are still less well known.

Central to the idea of a Protestant International in the way I am constructing it is an implicit and explicit repudiation of the "Christendom model," namely the notion of a Christian society maintained by an alliance of church and state against which the voluntary religious networks of the early modern period struggled. Hugh Mcleod states that for the fifteen hundred years after Constantine declared Christianity as the official religion of the Roman Empire in 312:

[1] Christopher Clark and Michael Ledger-Lomas, "The Protestant International," in Abigail Green and Vincent Viaene (eds.), *Religious Internationals in the Modern World* (London, 2012), 23–24.
[2] Kathleen Carté, *Religion and the American Revolution: An Imperial History* (Chapel Hill, 2021), 2.

most Christians learnt and practiced their faith in the context of "Christendom." That is, they lived in a society where there were close ties between the leaders of the church and those in positions of secular power, where the laws purported to be based on Christian principles, and where, apart from certain clearly defined outsider communities, every member of the society was assumed to be a Christian.[3]

In practice, the "Christendom model" was often characterized by state-enforced legal and political penalties against those outside established churches, territorially based ecclesiastical units for Christianizing local populations, and a determination to minimize dissidence and dissent in religious belief and practice.

I begin with a personal story. It is more than a decade since the passing of William Reginald Ward, arguably the greatest historian of the Protestant International. I first came across Professor Ward's work as a young graduate student in St. Andrews University almost at the beginning of his prolific Thirty Years' War of writing religious history in opposition to what he considered to be the then dominant paradigms constructed by Anglican chauvinists, Marxist reductionists, sentimental religious ecumenists, and parochial Anglo-American religious historians. Although he had already built a distinguished career as a historian on other subjects,[4] his book on

---

[3] Hugh McLeod and Werner Ustorf, *The Decline of Christendom in Western Europe, 1750–2000* (Cambridge, 2003), 1. For an example of how Christendom functioned in a particular time and place and how it was beginning to be challenged, see David Hempton, "Religion in British Society," in Jeremy Black (ed.), *British Politics from Walpole to Pitt 1742–1789* (London, 1990), 201–21.

[4] Most notably on the history of Oxford University and the operation of the land tax in England and Scotland.

Religion and Society in England 1790–1850, published in
1972, was his first serious foray into the world of popular evangelicalism, and what a foray it turned out to be.
I can still remember its first sentence, which dropped off
the page like an intellectual time bomb. "The generation
overshadowed by the French Revolution," he wrote, "was
the most important generation in the modern history
not only of English religion, but of most of the Christian
world. For the Revolution altered forever the terms on
which religious establishments, the chief device on which
the nations of the West had relied for christianising the
people must work."[5] Ward's thesis was that by 1790 a
non-denominational evangelical Protestantism, with
Methodism in the leading role and influenced by "enlightened" ideas, was poised to reshape the old denominational orders in nations right across the north Atlantic
world and beyond. This prospect was destroyed in the
British Isles, but not in the United States, by the French
Revolution which assigned religion the role of keeping
social order in desperate times. In Britain the Methodists,
with Jabez Bunting at the helm, cozied up to the established order and inexorably quenched the revival, while
in the United States populist evangelicals of all stripes
literally did refashion the old denominational order, the
consequences of which for the new Republic should not
be underestimated.[6]

[5] W. R. Ward, *Religion and Society in England, 1790–1850* (London,
1972), 1.
[6] For the transatlantic dimensions to the rise of Methodism and
its consequences, see David Hempton, *Methodism: Empire of the
Spirit* (New Haven, 2005). See also John Wolffe, *The Expansion of
Evangelicalism: The Age of Wilberforce, More, Chalmers and Finney*

Ward's book was a time bomb because, in his typical swashbuckling style, he cut the ground from under both E. P. Thompson's portrayal of Methodism as a proletarian disease and Owen Chadwick's magisterial, but smugly Anglican, airbrushing of English religion during the Industrial Revolution.[7] Ward's chosen vantage point from which to look at religion in the age of revolutions was not through the intellectual elites of London, Berlin, or Paris, but rather the evangelical radicals of Manchester, the first great shock city of the Industrial Revolution. Since writing that book, it is almost as if Ward placed the point of his compass in the "dark satanic mills" of the North of England and started to draw a series of ever widening geographical and chronological circles that took him back in time and far beyond the shores of the British Isles.[8] In a string of important books, and equally important but less-well-known articles, some of which were collected in *Faith and Faction*, Ward, the self-confessed old Primitive Methodist Ranter, traveled in search of the roots of evangelical Protestantism, the reasons for its spectacular early successes, and, in his opinion, its rather sorry condition by the end of the nineteenth century.[9] He constructed a trilogy of breathtaking intellectual scope and depth,

(Downers Grove, Ill, 2007). For the impact of popular evangelicalism on the new Republic, see Nathan O. Hatch, *The Democratization of American Christianity* (New Haven, 1989) and Daniel Walker Howe, *What God Hath Wrought: The Transformation of America, 1815–1848* (New York, 2007).

[7] E. P. Thompson, *The Making of the English Working Class* (London, 1968); Owen Chadwick, *The Victorian Church* (London, 1966–70).

[8] Charles Hubert Hastings Parry (1848–1918), "Jerusalem" (public domain).

[9] W. R. Ward, *Faith and Faction* (London, 1993).

beginning with *The Protestant Evangelical Awakening*, followed by *Christianity under the Ancien Régime 1648–1789*, and completed by *Early Evangelicalism: A Global Intellectual History, 1670–1789.*[10] The main argument of this trilogy is that in Europe after Westphalia religion was too important a matter to be left entirely to the churches. Most rulers before the late eighteenth century regarded religious toleration as a sign of state weakness and relied principally upon established churches to enforce conformity and order.[11] But the established churches, which had worked so hard for their place in the political sun, soon found themselves in unexpected difficulties. Some rulers coveted their wealth, while the churches themselves struggled, unsuccessfully as it happened, to find sufficient resources to cope with rapidly expanding populations. Disappointed mutual expectations resulted in clashes between religious and secular authorities, which were played out with equal bitterness in many different regions, from the disputes over patronage in Scotland to the almost relentless sniping between French kings and the papacy throughout the entire period. The inability of established churches to align their resources with their objectives or to eradicate popular superstition left them creaking audibly in the generation after the Seven Years' War (1756–63). Creaking became groaning in the 1790s when the revolutionaries

---

[10] W. R. Ward, *The Protestant Evangelical Awakening* (Cambridge, 1992); *Christianity under the Ancien Régime 1648–1789* (Cambridge, 1999); *Early Evangelicalism: A Global Intellectual History, 1670–1789* (Cambridge, 2006).

[11] See Benjamin J. Kaplan, *Divided by Faith: Religious Conflict and the Practice of Toleration in Early Modern Europe* (Cambridge, MA, 2007).

summarily dealt with the French church and the English church began to lose its affinity with national sentiment that had once been its glory. Although it took time for the various historical processes to play out, established churches everywhere, including the Celtic fringes of the British Isles, would never be the same again.[12]

Meanwhile, a new and dynamic religious movement, evangelical revivalism, was helping to transform the "Protestant Interest" of post-Reformation states and dynasties into a "Protestant International," which did not depend on support from established interests in church and state. Revivalism in the Habsburg lands was the response of pious minorities who had to achieve quick results or else go under. Often with no time to wait for church renewal or, more likely, with no institutional church to renew, Moravians, Silesians, and Saltzburgers pioneered new forms of popular Protestantism and exported them to Western Europe and then to the Americas. Class meetings began with Spener in 1670; camp meetings originated with the Swedish army in Silesia in the early eighteenth century; and itinerant preaching developed as a survival strategy for pietist communities. All was accompanied by a phenomenal increase in hymn writing and by revivals instituted and conducted by children. The money behind the expansion came from the commercial exploitation of medicaments, Bibles, and religious literature, and from the availability of Dutch credit at low rates of interest. Indeed, Ward was one of the few historians to take seriously the importance of the financing of religious

---

[12] W. R. Ward, *Religion and Society in England 1790–1850* (London, 1971), 1–6.

ventures. How money was raised and how it was spent, including debt retirement, is a vital but under-researched aspect of religious history.

It is perhaps Ward's most important achievement to show that whereas established churches were creaking from accumulated lethargy, Protestant Christianity, at least for a couple of generations, "exhibited astonishing new vigor by going over wholesale to unconfessional, international, societary means of action, in which the laity paid for and often ran great machines which had no place in the traditional church orders."[13] From Methodism to the great Protestant missionary societies of the nineteenth century, the pietism of a mobilized laity achieved remarkable feats of gospel transmission through voluntary networks across the transatlantic world and beyond.

The third and last book of Ward's trilogy focused on the intellectual and cultural origins of evangelicalism and on the core of evangelical identity, or the nucleus in our parlance, which characterized all the major strands of evangelicalism, from Halle to Northampton, Massachusetts, and with all the many stops in between. Though often bitterly divided over both belief and practice, evangelical Protestants nevertheless constructed a global fraternity around a number of important themes. These themes – "the close association with mysticism, the small-group religion, the deferred eschatology, the experimental approach to conversion, anti-Aristotelianism and hostility to theological system, and the attempt to reinforce religious vitality by setting it in the context of a vitalist understanding of nature … formed a sort of evangelical

---

[13] Ward, *Christianity under the Ancien Régime 1648–1789*, 250.

115

hexagon lasting until the original evangelical cohesion began to fail."[14] By the end of the nineteenth century a less expansive evangelicalism emerged, this time constructed around biblical inerrancy, pre-millennial dispensationalism, propositional systems of all kinds, and bureaucratic denominationalism. An infallible text read with wooden literalism, an instant millennium, an absence of mystery, a lack of interest in nature, priestly personality cults, and modernist soteriological systems, according to Ward, were not what the early evangelicals had in mind.

What Ward has shown is that what we call evangelicalism arose out of a quite specific historical context in post Thirty Years' War Europe, drew from a surprisingly eclectic intellectual culture, coalesced for a time around a number of important "shapers" or "themes," was disseminated internationally through sweeping population movements and by revivalists who knew of each other's labors, and changed over time and from place to place as a result of social and intellectual pressures.

The essence of Ward's argument is that in the period between Westphalia and the French Revolution, state persecution, sweeping population movements, the rise of voluntary organizations, and the pastoral and political limitations of established churches produced major changes in transnational Protestantism from the Urals in the east to the Appalachians in the west, and then to the rest of the world through ubiquitous missionary societies. The era of the French Revolution accelerated some of those changes and gave them an even wider

---

[14] Ward, *Early Evangelicalism*, 4.

geographical salience. A prime example was the growth of Protestant interest in converting the wider world. The period between 1790 and 1815 saw the formation of a remarkable wave of new Protestant missionary societies: the Baptist Missionary Society (1792), the (London) Missionary Society (1795), the Edinburgh (Scottish) and Glasgow Missionary Societies (1796), the Society for Missions to Africa and the East (1796, and known as the Church Missionary Society from 1812), and the Wesleyan Methodist Missionary Society in 1813. The British societies also connected with a host of continental European missionary societies with Lutheran, Reformed, Moravian, and pietist roots in Germany, Switzerland, and the Netherlands. The formation of the London Missionary Society led, across the Atlantic, directly to the formation of the New York Missionary Society and its sister organization, the Northern Missionary Society in the State of New York. They were followed by a flurry of new missionary organizations, including the Berkshire and Columbia Missionary Society (1798), the Missionary Society of Connecticut (1798), the Massachusetts Missionary Society (1799), the New Hampshire Missionary Society (1801), the Hampshire Missionary Society (1802), the Massachusetts Baptist Missionary Society (1802), the Presbyterian Standing Commission of Missions (1802), and the Western Missionary Society (1802).[15] The American societies were mostly Congregational, Presbyterian, and Baptist and located in New England, and they initially concentrated their attention on frontier

---

[15] I am grateful to my doctoral student, Thomas Whittaker, for information on the American "Missionary Republic."

church planting and Indian missions. Despite the limited geographical range of their work, the members of these societies understood themselves to be participating in a worldwide missionary movement of the Spirit, and the American missionary periodicals frequently published missionary intelligence from Europe.

The sheer scale of this voluntaristic surge of interest in missions across the globe, replete with their subscription lists, missionary intelligence, prayer networks, female auxiliaries, and widely distributed pamphlets, in such a short space of time, takes some explaining. In part, these networks were constructed on top of, or influenced by, earlier traditions, especially the remarkably influential missionary exploits of the Halle pietists and the Moravians. The latter had been active in international missions since the 1730s and were important connectors with other evangelicals in the 1780s and 1790s through their writings on missions and the publication of the quarterly *Periodical Accounts* in the spring of 1790, which was "the first missionary journal to appear at regular intervals and to be devoted entirely to missionary news."[16] The *Periodical Accounts* circulated widely among leaders of all the other missionary societies and made its way across the Atlantic through preexisting Moravian settlements and networks.[17]

---

[16] J. C. S. Mason, *The Moravian Church and the Missionary Awakening in England 1760–1800* (London, 2001), 180–81.

[17] See the circulation list in Mason, *The Moravian Church*, 202–4. As well as the *Periodical Accounts Relating to the Missions of the Church of the United Brethren Established among the Heathen*, there were a number of influential pamphlets on mission published in the 1780s and 1790s. See, for example, A. G. Spangenberg, *An Account of the Manner in which the Protestant Church of the Unitas Fratum, or United Brethren, Preach the Gospel, and Carry on their Missions among the Heathen*

118

However important the Moravians were as catalysts of other Protestant missionary ventures, there were many additional factors contributing to the growing interest in international missions. The French Revolution provoked both alarm and excitement for British and European Protestants alternatively pleased with a potentially fatal blow struck at the French Roman Catholic Church and fearful of the spread of revolutionary Jacobinism as Napoleon's armies marched across Europe. It is striking how often continental missionary societies were either started or revitalized by the incipient approach of French troops.[18] In this way, the Protestant missionary international was an alternative global ideology, a rival cosmopolitanism with its metropolitan base in London, and soon New York, to the "Rights of Man" with its metropolitan center in Paris.

There were, of course, other factors at play in London's emergence as an important node in the Protestant missionary international. The growing influence of evangelicals in British public life coincided with, and partly created, deep unease about sin and virtue in Britain's emerging empire in India and with the nation's participation in the transatlantic slave trade.[19] Not surprisingly, with such profound issues at stake the surge of interest in missions

(London, 1788); William Carey, *An Enquiry into the Obligations of Christians, to Use Means for the Conversion of the Heathens. In which the Religious State of the Different Nations of the World, the Success of Former Undertakings, and the Practicability of Further Undertakings are Considered* (Leicester, 1792); and Melville Horne, *Letters on Missions; Addressed to the Protestant Ministers of British Churches* (Bristol, 1794).

[18] I owe this idea to Thomas Whittaker.

[19] Gareth Atkins, *Converting Britannia: Evangelicals and British Public Life, 1770–1840* (Woodbridge, Suffolk, 2019).

was accompanied by a parallel surge of interest in biblicist millennialism, of both the optimistic variety emphasizing the millennial advance of the Gospel and also a more pessimistic, but equally energetic, premillennial version that interpreted the signs of the times as so grim that only the returning Christ could save the godly from further trials and tribulations. Both theological versions could be pessimistic about the sinful state of the world, but also confident in the transforming power of the Gospel. In different ways, as either ushering in a global harvest of souls or urgently rescuing a remnant for the returning Christ, missions stood to benefit from both. In the era of the French Revolution, British, continental European, and American evangelical Protestants mobilized an army of voluntary networks with nodes in London, Basel, Berlin, New York, and Boston to propagate the Gospel across the world and resist the evils of Jacobinism, slavery, Romanism, and infidelity. In Britain and Europe, success was to be measured in the confrontation with revolutionary France and at the edges of empire; in the American Republic, the destiny of the new nation was to be decided in the West, among Western settlers and Indigenous peoples. The stakes for the Protestant International could hardly have been higher or its geographical scope more extensive. It could appeal simultaneously to national renewal and international transformation.

At the same time as the Protestant global missionary mobilization was taking place, and for some of the same reasons, including heightened anxiety provoked by the age of revolutions, especially the French, another dimension to the Protestant International was taking shape with equally important consequences, namely the remarkable proliferation of interest in apocalypticism. It is well known that the generation overshadowed by the French Revolution throughout the Protestant world began ransacking their Scriptures for apocalyptic clues about the end times and that millenarians of all hues, from Millerites, Mormons, and Adventists in the United States to predominantly established church evangelicals and popular enthusiasts in the British Isles, displayed an unprecedented interest in biblical prophecy. Of course, interest in the end times, including a renewed interest in what was to be the fate of the Jews and the various ways of interpreting the second coming of Jesus and the biblical millennium, were not new features of the Christian tradition in the early nineteenth century. What was new was the transatlantic proliferation of prophecy conferences, periodicals, and publications devoted to parsing out the biblical prophecies and relating them to actual historical events – past, present, and future. In addition, this generic interest in apocalypticism morphed over time into a coherent, if imaginatively expansive, theological system that was successfully disseminated across the North Atlantic world and became a key component of what later became known as fundamentalism. At stake here is no mere passing interest in esoteric and exotic biblicist fantasies, but rather the uncovering of one of the most powerful cultural shapers of the American Republic.[20] For example, a recent book on *Religion and the Rise of Capitalism* by an eminent economist devotes

---

[20] For a recent and reliable deep dive into prophetical ideas and literature and their significant impact on American culture, see Daniel G. Hummel, *The Rise and Fall of Dispensationalism: How the Evangelical Battle over the End Times Shaped a Nation* (Grand Rapids, MI, 2023).

considerable space to elucidating the importance of the nineteenth-century conflict between post- and premillennialism, and explains its long-term consequences for ideas about economic progress and later the fusion of conservative religious, political, and economic worldviews in modern America.[21] Its basic argument is that the economic ideas constructed by Adam Smith, "with its self-contained dynamic theory about how an economy advances from one way of meeting human needs to the next, was strikingly congruent with the postmillennialist thinking put forward by a series of English theologians over the prior two centuries." In short, Smith's conceptions of economic advance were developed at a time and place when trends in theology were moving away from predestinarian Calvinism with its emphasis on human depravity and were consonant with postmillennialist views of human agency and progress.[22]

The organizing framework of these lectures – namely nuclei, nodes, and networks in the transmission of religious ideas, movements, and cultures – is especially useful for understanding the roots and transnational dissemination of apocalyptic theologies and ideologies. As Ernest Sandeen pointed out in a pathbreaking book half a century ago, there were multiple streams of apocalypticism in Britain and the United States in the first one-third of the nineteenth century, but what he called "the basic tenets of the millenarian creed" were held with surprising unanimity:

[21] Benjamin M. Friedman, *Religion and the Rise of Capitalism* (New York, 2021).
[22] Friedman, *Religion and the Rise of Capitalism*, 232.

the belief that acceptance of the divine authority of Scripture required that the believer expect a literal rather than a spiritual fulfillment of the prophecies; the belief that the gospel was not intended to nor was it going to accomplish the salvation of the world, but that, instead the world was growing increasingly corrupt and rushing towards imminent judgment; the belief that Christ would literally return to this earth and the Jews be restored to Palestine before the commencement of the millennial age;

and above all that all this was discoverable by sincere believers from careful readings of the Scriptures.[23] Stating what was shared, however, should not diminish the importance of what was not shared. Although there were countless variations played out in the ubiquitous millenarian publications and periodicals over the course of the nineteenth century, there was a fundamental division between postmillennialists and what have been called "new premillennialists" (distinguishing them from older Christian traditions), and within the latter category between historicists and futurists. Historicists believed that the biblical prophecies contained in the Books of Daniel and Revelation were intricately connected and that most of these prophecies had already been fulfilled, while futurists believed that none of the events predicted in the Book of Revelation had yet been fulfilled. This may seem a distinction without a substantial difference, but the difference was that many of the premillennial historicists of the nineteenth century, including William Miller, specialized not only in matching the biblical days and

---

[23] Ernest R. Sandeen, *The Roots of Fundamentalism: British and American Millenarianism, 1800–1930* (Chicago, 1970), 39.

years to real historical events, but also, on the basis of their calculations, came up with quite specific dates for the physical second coming of Jesus. David Morgan has shown how Millerites and others built on earlier traditions of prophetical images to construct elaborate charts, literally mapping time, which were widely disseminated in the Jacksonian age of explosive growth of newspapers, periodicals, handbills, and broadsides. Adventist charts brought together in accessible form the aesthetic power of images, the sacrosanct authority of the Bible, a vivid interpretation and organization of historical events, and a place for devoted followers to find meaning and significance within the great scope of human history and eternity.[24] But, as all historians know, interpreting the past is one thing; predicting the future is quite another, and as we all now know, all of the predicted dates for the second coming, including the Millerites' and many others on both sides of the Atlantic, turned out to be wrong or in serious need of imaginative tweaking. Not surprisingly, therefore, over the course of the nineteenth century, premillennial historicists gradually gave way to futurists, whose temporal claims lay in the future and therefore could not be so easily falsified.

One particular strand of premillennialism, the dispensational scheme incorporating the future rapture of the saints constructed by the Anglo-Irish clergyman John Nelson Darby, has had a cultural impact way beyond its quite humble roots.[25] The node or "inception site" in

---

[24] David Morgan, *Protestants and Pictures: Religion, Visual Culture, and the Age of American Mass Production* (New York, 1999), 123–58.
[25] In Hummel's *The Rise and Fall of Dispensationalism*, he makes a distinction between "dispensational" and "dispensationalism," which

this unlikely story is County Wicklow and south County Dublin in the 1820s and 1830s, when a group of evangelical Church of Ireland clergymen, with the help of aristocratic and gentry patronage, organized conferences on biblical prophecy on the Powerscourt estate. The context is important. It was already clear that the so-called "Second Reformation" movement of the 1820s to convert Irish Catholics to Protestantism, despite self-serving propaganda to the contrary, had largely failed, and it had become obvious from Daniel O'Connell's Campaign for Catholic Emancipation that the Anglo-Irish Protestant ascendancy was living on borrowed time. Not surprisingly, a political and clerical caste aware of its own impending defeat, but still persuaded of the truth of its Protestant religious tradition, looked to its sacred texts for guidance and direction. Apocalyptic speculation in times of stress and strain is of course not a new feature of the Christian tradition; what was new about Ireland in the 1830s was the emergence of a particularly forceful and energetic personality, John Nelson Darby, who constructed an imaginatively compelling history of time – past, present, and future – shaped by a literalist interpretation of the Bible. What were these ideas?

According to Donald Akenson in two important books on the Darbyite phenomenon, *Discovering the End of Time* and *Exporting the Rapture*, Darby and his coterie of Wicklow-Dublin supporters brought together a rigorous re-examination of biblical prophecies with a set

he contends is a term not used until 1927 (by Philip Mauro) and which anachronistically imposes a degree of homogenization on a notoriously disparate and fissiparous set of ideas.

of historical and contemporary observations about the dismal state of the Protestant churches to construct "a fecund constellation of ideas, beliefs and practices" that came to have a disproportionate influence on transatlantic evangelicalism.[26] These included a revolutionary reframing of theology based on "an extremely literalistic reading of big swaths of the Bible that orthodox churches read allegorically; a belief that Jesus would physically appear on earth; an interpretation of biblical prophecy that affirmed it to be, when read properly, a precise map of how the road would run from Jesus's return onward into deep eternity."[27] In that mode, Darby affirmed the secret rapture of the saints and took a literal view of the Tribulation, Armageddon, and the millennium. This was both imaginatively inventive and deeply conservative (rooted in ancient scriptural texts), a compelling *story* of a divine and human drama, not a theological *treatise*, a way of ordering time from creation to the last judgment, and a repivoting of Christian and human history away from the crucifixion and resurrection of Jesus to some future rapture and second advent. According to Akenson, Darby and his colleagues were attempting nothing less than "a rearrangement of two of Western cultures fundamental texts: the Hebrew and the Christian scriptures. Eventually they melded together the two texts in totally

---

[26] Donald Harman Akenson, *Discovering the End of Time: Irish Evangelicals in the Age of Daniel O'Connell* (Montreal & Kingston, 2016); *Exporting the Rapture: John Nelson Darby and the Victorian Conquest of North-American Evangelicalism* (New York, 2018). See also Harold H. Rowdon, *The Origins of the Brethren 1825–1850* (London, 1967); F. Roy Coad, *A History of the Brethren Movement: Its Origins, Its Worldwide Development, and Its Significance for the Present Day* (Exeter, 1968).

[27] Akenson, *Exporting the Rapture*, 43.

new ways, so different from previous arrangements as to *constitute a new Bible.*"[28]

If the node in this story was the coterie of radical Irish evangelicals in southern Ireland in the 1820s and 1830s and the nucleus is the emerging dispensational premillennial scheme of human history and human destiny constructed by them, the networks of transmission still await rigorous historical treatment, though Akenson has supplied a roadmap from the life and travels of Darby himself.[29] The peripatetic Darby, though mostly located in southern England, from the later 1830s made frequent journeys to the Protestant environs of Western Europe, mostly Switzerland, France, and Germany. Moreover, since the Darbyite construction was as much ecclesiological as it was theological, the network of Exclusive Brethren and Brethren assemblies became delivery mechanisms of the new radical ideas. Darby himself visited North America seven times (as, coincidentally, did George Whitefield), comprising nearly seven years in all, between 1862 and 1877. Beginning first in the Great Lakes region of Canada and the United States, he later moved on to the great midwestern and east coast cities. Missionary journeys were augmented by prophecy and Bible conferences, some of which were inspired by Darby, such as at Guelph in Ontario, and others with more generic biblicist and millenarian origins such as those at Mildmay in

---

[28] Akenson, *Exporting the Rapture*, 49.
[29] See also Hummel, *The Rise and Fall of Dispensationalism*, ch. 2, "The American Mission Field," for a recent treatment of the dissemination of Darbyite ideas in the United States. Hummel's book is particularly useful in parsing out different stands of premillennial and dispensational theologies, which were enormously variegated.

England, Northfield and Niagara in North America, and countless others. The significance of the conferences and Bible institutes are that they allowed transatlantic, almost exclusively male, evangelical networks to come together in ways that traditional denominationalism did not easily permit. Planning committees, conference speakers, correspondence networks, editorial boards, and coherence around systems of prophetical ideas based on scriptural exegesis and cultural analysis all sustained coteries of ministers and laymen in many different denominations and in multiple towns and cities throughout the British Isles and North America. In the United States these networks were trans-denominational, transcended social class, were not confined to specific regions, and were predominantly composed of comfortable white males who had the resources and know-how to travel.[30] Influential books and periodicals, populist preachers, formidable tract distribution networks, prophetical diagrams, and newly written hymns kept the prophetical ideas moving along the networks. Edward Bishop Elliott's *Horae Apocalypticae* was published in 1844, the *Theological and Literary Journal* was first published in 1848, Horatio Bonar's *Quarterly Journal of Prophecy* first appeared in 1849, and the *Prophetic Times*, a monthly periodical, began in 1863. These were among the most influential, but there were scores of others, not to mention the prophetical items in many of the specifically denominational periodicals. Most of the circulating literature on prophecy was premillennial and increasingly futurist, with ongoing controversies around Darbyite

---

[30] See Matthew Avery Sutton, *American Apocalypse: A History of Modern Evangelicalism* (Cambridge, MA, 2014), 2–3.

interpretations which attracted both loyal support and critical opprobrium. Darby's ideas were given a massive boost by the publication of the *Scofield Reference Bible* in 1909, the best-selling Oxford University Press book of all time, which popularized and democratized the premillennial dispensational scheme in accessible form. Moving into the later twentieth century, Hal Lindsay's immensely popular *The Late Great Planet Earth* and the *Left Behind* novels, which have collectively sold more than sixty million copies,[31] delivered premillennial dispensationalism into the populist bloodstream of American evangelical Protestantism with incalculable consequences for the religious, political, and cultural history of the nation.[32]

Immersing oneself in this biblical literalist, prophetical literature, it is hard to resist the conclusion that it operated as a kind of male, English-speaking book club, with the Bible as the book and the prophecies operating as clues to unlocking the secret history of time. The cultural charge many brought to this transatlantic club was a deep-seated cultural pessimism about what was happening in the world around them, not always without foundation, together with an equally deep-seated sense of chosen destiny as saints armed with the right keys to unlock the mysteries from which they and they alone would be the beneficiaries. Such views often produced urgency and activism, as well as a sense of being part of a divine plan accessible only to faithful students

---

[31] Hal Lindsay with C. C. Carlson, *The Late Great Planet Earth* (Grand Rapids, 1970); Tim LaHaye and Jerry B. Jenkins, *Left Behind* series (Carol Stream, IL, 1995–2007).
[32] Barry Hankins (ed.), *Evangelicalism and Fundamentalism: A Documentary Reader* (New York, 2008), 59–70.

of biblical prophecies. Naturally, critics, both within the existing Protestant denominations and even more stringently those outside, thought very differently. Among the most savage of the critics was George Eliot, who vented her spleen on Dr. Cumming, the minister of the Crown Court Presbyterian Church in London and prolific publisher of books on biblical prophecy:

> You might as well attempt to educate a child's sense of beauty by hanging its nursery with the horrible and grotesque pictures in which the early painters represented the Last Judgment, as expect Christian graces to flourish on that prophetic interpretation which Dr Cumming offers as the principal nutriment of his flock ... advertising the premillennial Advent is simply the transportation of political passions on to a so-called religious platform; it is the anticipation of the triumph of "our party" accomplished by our principal men being "sent for" into the clouds ... It would be idle to consider Dr Cumming's theory of prophecy in any other light, – as a philosophy of history or a specimen of Biblical interpretation; it bears about the same relation to the extension of genuine knowledge as the astrological "house" in the heavens bears to the true structure and relations of the universe.[33]

Eliot's criticism of Cumming's theological worldview is an early example of modernist distaste for the kind of "fundamentalism" that grew out of premillennial and dispensational apocalypticism. Indeed, she uses the phrase "fundamental faith," not to describe Cumming, but to pose a different worldview based on what she called the brave, honest, and steady use of all

[33] George Eliot, "Evangelical Teaching: Dr Cumming," in *Essays and Leaves from a Note-Book* (London, 1884), 182–85.

human faculties to amplify "the tendency towards good in human nature."[34]

The roots of American fundamentalism were deep and extensive long before the publication of *The Fundamentals* between 1910–15 and the formation of the World's Christian Fundamentals Association in Philadelphia in 1919. They encompass resistance to the three Rs of rationalism, romanism, and ritualism; hostility to modernism, theological liberalism, and biblical criticism; forebodings of the threats posed by scientific naturalism (especially Darwinism) and urbanization; anxiety about heresies from within; and finally fear of the international challenges of ecumenism, socialism, and communism. The strand that we have followed from the generation overshadowed by the American and French Revolutions to the early twentieth century, dispensational premillennialism, is a major part of the story. According to George Marsden, a powerful group of leaders emerged in the later decades of the nineteenth century, including Dwight L. Moody, Reuben A. Torrey, C. I. Scofield, William Erdman, and A. J. Gordon, who gave institutional permanence to the dispensational movement through the new Bible institutes such as the Moody Bible Institute (1886), the Bible Institute of Los Angeles (1907), and the Philadelphia College of the Bible (1914). He writes that "the network of related institutes that soon sprang up became the nucleus for much of the fundamentalist movement of the twentieth century."[35] Not all fundamentalists in

---

[34] Eliot, "Evangelical Teaching: Dr Cumming," 199.
[35] George M. Marsden, *Understanding Fundamentalism and Evangelicalism* (Grand Rapids, 1991), 40–41. See also David W. Bebbington, *The Dominance of Evangelicalism: The Age of Spurgeon and Moody* (Downers

the 1920s and beyond were premillennial dispensationalists, but all premillennial dispensationalists were fundamentalists. Although beyond the scope of this chapter,
it is hard to overstate the influence of fundamentalism
on American evangelicalism, especially in the Southern
states after World War Two, and especially after 1960. It
is equally hard to understate the impact of that reformu-
lated evangelicalism on the cultural and political history
of the United States and the rise of the Moral Majority
and Christian nationalism from the election of Ronald
Reagan to the election of Donald Trump.[36]

Some of the same structural forces that were at work in
producing premillennial dispensationalism and later fundamentalism were also operational in the emergence of
probably the most important movement of Christianity
since the Reformation: Pentecostalism. Indeed, one of
the most influential contributors to the writings and conferences on prophecy in the 1820s was Edward Irving, the
Scottish minister of the Caledonian Chapel in London,
who found himself at the center of controversy in 1831
after the apparent manifestation of the apostolic gift
of tongues in his church. Prior to that, there had been
reports of miraculous healings and tongue-speaking in
western Scotland in 1830, persuading Irving that the
long-anticipated outpouring of the gifts of the Holy Spirit

Grove, IL, 2005); Mark A. Noll, *A History of Christianity in the United States and Canada* (Grand Rapids, MI, 1992), ch. 14.

[36] For recent interpretations of this important story, see Randall Balmer, *Evangelicalism in America* (Waco, Texas, 2016) and Frances Fitzgerald, *The Evangelicals: The Struggle to Shape America* (New York, 2017). For an insightful account of the rise of Christian nationalism, see Tim Alberta, *The Kingdom, the Power, and the Glory: American Evangelicals in an Age of Extremism* (New York, 2023).

was at hand. Space does not permit a review of Irving's meteoric and controversial career, which led to a heresy trial and an early death in 1834, but Irving anticipated by more than half a century the Pentecostal explosion of the early twentieth century. The question is, to what extent is this most recent expression of the Protestant International amenable to explanations arising from our organizing principles of networks, nodes, and nuclei?

Let us start at the beginning. Grant Wacker, in the best treatment of early Pentecostalism in American culture, locates the origins of American Pentecostalism in four streams that had been flowing through the American religious landscape for many decades: "Partisans channeled each of these theological streams – personal salvation, Holy Ghost baptism (in Wesleyan holiness, Oberlin perfectionist, and Keswick higher-life forms), divine healing, and dispensational premillennialism – through a vast institutional network. That network included conferences, summer camps, books, magazines, colleges, Bible institutes, and a web of national, regional, and local associations."[37] In short, the rise of Pentecostalism is unintelligible without a grasp of the full extent of the *networks* created by radical evangelical subcultures out of which it emerged at the beginning of the twentieth century. These networks operated before, during, and after instances of pentecostal awakenings and help explain their transmission beyond a single site or even a single country. As for the nucleus of Pentecostalism, most would locate it in the experience of Holy Spirit baptism

---

[37] Grant Wacker, *Heaven Below: Early Pentecostals and American Culture* (Cambridge, MA, 2001), 3.

and the spiritual gifts accompanying it, but Wacker, while not denying the centrality of spirit baptism, finds the essence of Pentecostalism in a combination of primitivism and pragmatism – a direct unfiltered experience of divine power and intimacy on the one hand and a realistic grasp of temporal realities and necessities on the other. Moreover, focusing on what Pentecostals shared as lived experience helps explain why first-generation adherents in the American South often had more in common with Pentecostals in other parts of the country than with their non-Pentecostal southern neighbors.[38]

What, then, of the nodes, or junction boxes, of Pentecostal transmission, which of course raises controversial issues of historical origins and American/Western imperialism? My framing metaphor and analytical framework is borrowed from one of the most empathetic and insightful books on global Pentecostalism, David Martin's *Pentecostalism: The World Their Parish*. In his first chapter, entitled "A Cultural Revolution," Martin traces the origins of Pentecostalism to the "unsponsored mobilizations of *laissez-faire* lay religion, running to and fro between Britain and North America, especially between their respective unruly margins in Ulster, Cornwall, Scotland, and Wales, and in Kentucky, Kansas, Texas, and (finally) California." He suggests that through these trails American experimental religion marched alongside

---

[38] See Randall Stephens, *The Fire Spreads: Holiness and Pentecostalism in the American South* (Cambridge, MA, 2010), 13. Stephens states that southern Pentecostals "seldom identified with the shibboleths of sectionalism" and came to "think of themselves as part of a larger religious family or a translocal community that obliterated many sectional, class, and racial barriers."

American modernization and produced "a potent variable capable of stomping alongside modernization worldwide. It met life-threatening and feckless disorder with personal discipline and collective ecstasy." Then comes the metaphor. "What happened following the explosive star-burst at the end of the trail in Los Angeles in 1906, and equally following all the other parallel star-bursts world-wide, was a hurling of people in every direction, carrying with them a fusion of the faith of culturally despised poor blacks with that of culturally despised poor whites."[39] The picture is of a crescendo to a fireworks display when rockets from different sources explode in bright lights and send countless smoky streamers ending in infinite numbers of other star-bursts. This image has also been employed to illustrate multiple new expressions and new locations of Pentecostalism right down through the twentieth century, which cannot reasonably

[39] David Martin, *Pentecostalism: The World Their Parish* (Oxford, 2002), 5. See also Harvey Cox, *Fire from Heaven: The Rise of Pentecostal Spirituality and the Reshaping of Religion in the Twenty-first Century* (New York, 1995). Grant Wacker and some others think that the image of early Pentecostals as destitute migrant laborers may be overdrawn. Also, in their ranks were mostly stable industrial and farm workers and aspiring lower middle-class service workers. Generally speaking, the historiography of Pentecostalism has followed a similar trajectory to other forms of populist Protestantism, beginning with hagiographic accounts by insiders, often followed by critical treatments from professional historians emphasizing social class and dislocation (for example, Robert Mapes Anderson's classic, *Vision of the Disinherited: The Making of American Pentecostalism* [New York, 1979]), provoking a counter narrative from more empathetic historians paying greater attention to actual beliefs and practices as well as social contexts. More recently, Western-centered approaches have been challenged by accounts from the Global South, where Pentecostalism has achieved greater depth of penetration.

be attributed to a singular "Big Bang theory of global Pentecostalism," but rather to a string of firecrackers, with each new bang "separated from the others in time and space" and representing "a diffusive center for new Pentecostal-charismatic ideas or practices."[40]

All metaphors have their limits, and this one is no exception. What the burgeoning literature on global Pentecostalism shows beyond dispute is that it is no longer possible to claim that the Azusa Street revival in Los Angeles in 1906 is somehow the node and the nucleus from which all subsequent Pentecostal expressions in their dazzling complexity derived. In his helpful synthesis of scholarship on global Pentecostalism, *To the Ends of the Earth: Pentecostalism and the Transformation of World Christianity*, Allan Anderson shows that "although the Azusa Street revival was the most significant North American center of early Pentecostalism, it was neither the only one nor the earliest." There were various revivals in different parts of the world throughout the nineteenth century and in the critical first decade of the twentieth century which displayed "decidedly pentecostal characteristics, with gifts of the Spirit like healings, tongues, prophecy and other 'miraculous' signs."[41] Anderson

---

[40] Michael J. McClymond, Charismatic Renewal and Neo-Pentecostalism: From North America Origins to Global Permutations,' in Cecil M. Robeck, Jr. and Amos Young (eds.), *The Cambridge Companion to Pentecostalism* (New York, 2014), 44. This collection of essays mostly deals with historical origins, worldwide dissemination, and interdisciplinary approaches to explanations of Pentecostalism. See also Xi Lian, *Redeemed by Fire: The Rise of Popular Christianity in Modern China* (New Haven, 2010).

[41] Allan Heaton Anderson, *To the Ends of the Earth: Pentecostalism and the Transformation of Global Christianity* (Oxford, 2013), 19.

documents many localized revivals in different parts of the world in the nineteenth century in which spiritual gifts were manifested, including those associated with the Tamil evangelist John Christian Arulappan in Tamil Nadu in 1860–65 and others in nineteenth-century Russia, Armenia, and Estonia. Contemporary with the Azusa Street revival, but starting earlier and not directly influenced by it, there was tongue-speaking and prophesying in the Mukti revival associated with Pandita Ramabai, which in turn was influenced by the Australian revival of 1903 and the Welsh revival of 1904–05. Within a decade of Azusa Street there were revivals with pentecostal characteristics, but without known direct contacts with Los Angeles, in Korea, China, India, Chile, Nigeria, and Côte d'Ivoire. All this leads Anderson to conclude that Pentecostal origins are "complex and varied, polycentric, and diffused."[42] For these reasons, the burgeoning scholarship on global Pentecostalism, which according to some estimates embraces around a half a billion people worldwide, is appropriately wary of ceding hegemonic bragging rights to specific historical events on the west coast of the United States in the first decade of the twentieth century.[43] Pentecostalism became a global phenomenon partly because of its ability to adapt to local cultures in Latin America, sub-Saharan Africa, and Asia, in the same century and for some of the same reasons that Western imperialism, whether in

---

[42] Anderson, *To the Ends of the Earth*, 36.
[43] See, for example, Ogbu Kalu, *African Pentecostalism: An Introduction* (New York, 2008), which rejects the idea that Azusa Street should be the terminus point of all genealogies in favor of a Holy Spirit globalization without centers and peripheries.

its political or missionary versions, was coming under sustained opposition. Pentecostalism did not draw all its energy from anticolonial animus, but it could not have expanded so rapidly or established such deep roots without adaptation, indigenization, and acculturation in the age of decolonization. Adaptation and evolution, as with the coronaviruses with which we have now become all too familiar, produce endless new variants as host cultures reshape the DNA of the Pentecostal phenomenon. As its hugely variegated global expansion has demonstrated, Pentecostalism is eclectic, dynamic, pluralistic, and fissiparous. Indeed, Martin saw many parallels between Pentecostalism and the Methodist and Holiness traditions out of which it grew, including its capacity for schism and its tendency towards bureaucratization in its more established strongholds. But in essence, "Pentecostalism is not *a* church or any kind of system, but a repertoire of recognizable spiritual affinities which constantly breaks out in new forms" and in new places, which gives it the capacity to "break the moulds, above all in the huge population of the non-Western world."[44] The last phrase is important because Martin was convinced that "classical Pentecostalism is unlikely to be a major power in the developed world because it represents the mobilization of a minority of people at the varied margins of that world, whereas in the developing world it represents the mobilization of large masses."[45]

While it is important not to overstate the importance of Azusa Street as the foundational node of the

---

[44] Martin, *Pentecostalism*, 176.   [45] Martin, *Pentecostalism*, 67.

worldwide Pentecostal phenomenon for all of the reasons already alluded to, it is also unwise to understate its significance.[46] The various links in the chain of transmission of ideas connecting Spirit baptism and tongue-speaking (arguably the foundational nucleus of Pentecostalism), as conceived by Charles Fox Parham, and their application by the African-American preacher William Seymour at Azusa Street are well known, but the chain would not exist without the populist evangelical networks forged by Methodists, Holiness and healing preachers, Bible schools and missionary training institutes, premillennial pundits, and female leaders, some of whom have left traces while others have not. Moreover, Azusa Street was important for its melding of religious influences from African Americans, native Americans, lower class whites, and Latino migrants. It became the most prominent center of American (classical) Pentecostalism, partly because of its multiracial identity and controversial experiences and partly because of the influence of Seymour's periodical, *The Apostolic Faith*, which achieved an international circulation of more than 50,000 at its peak in 1908. Azusa Street also attracted large numbers of religious sightseers,

[46] For a detailed and sympathetic account of the Azusa Street revival which makes a case for its nodal centrality to global Pentecostalism, see Cecil M. Robeck, Jr., *The Azusa St Mission & Revival: The Birth of the Global Pentecostal Movement* (Nashville, 2006). In a concise summary of the book's argument, Robeck writes, "The Revival came to an African American congregation whose pastor [Seymour] had a vision for multiracial and multiethnic worship, which led them to salvation, sanctification, and baptism in the Holy Spirit. The revival did not stop there, but moved beyond the walls of the mission to the surrounding neighborhoods, across the nation, and around the world." 314.

of varying degrees of influence, and prolifically sent out missionaries to more than twenty-five countries in only two years.[47]

Azusa Street and the other Los Angeles satellites associated with it were not the only places on the North American continent where the Spirit touched down in the first decade of the twentieth century. There were other important early centers in New York, Chicago, and Toronto. Nor should it be regarded as causative or normative for Pentecostalism's global spread, but its role as a multiracial epicenter of the manifestation of spiritual gifts to quite humble people became important, even as a foundation myth, for Pentecostalism's multifaceted global expansion. Nevertheless, Azusa was the premier fountain for sending out missionaries who circled the globe surprisingly quickly. One of the reasons for this expansionist energy was the notion, almost unique to Azusa, that sometimes glossolalia was claimed to be xenolalia.

One aspect of Pentecostalism, which it shares with some earlier features of the Protestant International, is the importance of women as organizers, funders, and sustainers of family values and domestic disciplines against potential male flirtations with the sins of the flesh. Pentecostalism, like Methodism before it, was predominantly a women's movement, even if women were rarely given access to leadership positions or established pulpits.[48] Following the early women leaders of

---

[47] See Allan Anderson, *An Introduction to Pentecostalism* (Cambridge, 2004), 39–45, and Robeck, *The Azusa St Mission*, 235–80.
[48] For insightful treatments of women's roles in Pentecostalism, see Anderson, *To the Ends of the Earth*, 93–117, and Cheryl J. Sanders,

Pentecostalism tells one a great deal about the formal
and informal networks of where the movement came
from and how it developed. Of the twelve "apostles" who
functioned as a committee to license missionaries coming out of the Azusa Street revival, seven were women
and two were Black, and women were often pioneer
missionaries in various parts of the world. Some of the
biographies of prominent women, like Pandita Ramabai,
founder of the Mukti Mission in India, are well known,
but the life story of her close associate Minnie Abrams is
yet more revealing of the networks, early features, theologies, and geographical locations of the early Pentecostal
movement. "A classic example of the trajectory from
the women's missionary movement through holiness
to Pentecostalism," Abrams was born in Wisconsin
and attended the Methodist-related Chicago Training
School for Home and Foreign Missions founded and run
by Lucy Rider Meyer. Abrams went to India as a missionary of the Methodist Episcopal Church in 1887 and
left that position a decade later to work with the Mukti
Mission in Kedaon. As awareness spread of the 1904
Welsh Revival among mission stations, a Pentecostal
revival began at the Mukti Mission in the summer of
1905, the year before the Azusa Street revival. Abrams
brought together her Holiness spirituality, missionary
experience, and Spirit baptism in her book *The Baptism
of the Holy Ghost & Fire* (1906), which, through primarily female networks, became an important shaper
of Pentecostal mission theory, directly influencing the

*Saints in Exile: The Holiness-Pentecostal Experience in African American
Religion and Culture* (New York, 1996).

rise of Pentecostalism in Chile and other Pentecostal missions in China and Liberia.[49] Unfortunately, as with an earlier generation of female preachers within Methodism, once Pentecostalism was organized into denominations, formal leadership passed over to men, but in its pioneer phase Pentecostalism afforded new opportunities for women in leadership, partly because of its emphasis on the power of the Spirit, which gave women "a biblical rationale for cross-cultural evangelism and leadership, even in periods of time when the forces of fundamentalism and routinization tried to restrict the role of women."[50]

Minnie Abrams' life is traceable because she was educated at a notable training school for missionaries, was associated with one of the major "star-burst" revivals of early Pentecostalism in India, wrote one of its foundational texts, and influenced many other female missionaries to the three continents in which Pentecostalism exploded into vigorous life, but the networks she traveled along throughout her life were entirely characteristic of the Protestant International that shaped the lives of thousands of other less-well-documented women and men.

What, then, do we learn about the Protestant International through its networks, nodes, and nuclei? The first and most important is the centrality of the Bible

---

[49] See Dana L. Robert, *American Women in Mission: A Social History of Their Thought and Practice* (Macon, GA, 1997), 240–53. See also Dana L. Robert, *Christian Mission: How Christianity became a World Religion* (Chichester, 2009), 53–79.

[50] Robert, *American Women in Mission*, 253. For a fine biography of a female Pentecostal leader that also illuminates American Pentecostal subcultures, see Edith L. Blumhofer, *Aimee Semple McPherson: Everybody's Sister* (Grand Rapids, 1993).

and the divergent exegeses and novel theological constructions that came from reading it as a direct revelation of divine intentions for all humans. From the Reformation Anabaptists, through the dispensational premillennialists to the Pentecostal enthusiasts, the Bible was the window into the primitive church, the sword for resisting the coercion and condescension of Christendom's elites, and the key to unlocking the secrets of time and eternity.[51] Second is the importance of transnational and trans-denominational networks that do not easily give up their secrets unless embedded in institutions, publications, and correspondence. Yet these networks existed both formally and informally. Third is the impact of ubiquitous, mostly lay-led, voluntary societies and organizations and the influence of print culture in its manifold iterations – periodicals, tracts, pamphlets, and books. In the twentieth century, print culture was to some extent overtaken by radio and TV as the most significant bearers of the communication channels of popular Protestant transmission. Fourth is the reality that many of the most influential shapers of Protestantism over the past half a millennium started as critiques of the worldliness and pastoral mediocrity of established churches and denominations as insufficiently pure, zealous, or attentive to primitive Christianity. Fifth, the Protestant International has had an ambivalent relationship with its surrounding cultural contexts. On the one hand, it benefited from some of the most powerful cultural shapers of the early modern and modern eras, including liberal capitalism,

---

[51] See Mark A. Noll, *In the Beginning was the Word: The Bible in American Public Life, 1492–1783* (New York, 2016).

the rise of Protestant empires, and innovations in transport and technology; while on the other hand, there has been a relentless critique of cultural sins and a profound pessimism about the state of the world. Sixth, women are important to the whole enterprise and almost always comprise the majority of all popular Protestant communities, but they generally exercise more leadership at the beginning of new directions than at their end, when males create organizational structures to maintain control. Seventh, a nucleus of powerful ideas or memes has supplied a kind of nuclear fission in unleashing expansive energy. These include ideas such as the evangelistic commission to take the Gospel into all the world, or the belief in a physical second coming of Jesus around which the history of time is organized, or that through the baptism of the Holy Spirit unlimited power lies in the hands of all true believers. These ideas are no mere theological propositions around which orthodoxy is negotiated, but operate as powerful incentives to change the world. Eighth, populist Protestant traditions, because of their direct access to biblical interpretation, their critique of elite-run denominations, and their inexhaustible adaptation to fresh cultural settings, are notoriously fissiparous and vulnerable to power contests between authoritarian male leaders. Ninth, in the transmission of new theological ideas and forms of religious expression, it is important to pay attention to nodes and junction boxes – particular geographical or cultural sites – which supply the electrical energy in the transmission grid of international Protestantism. Finally, none of the transformations dealt with in this chapter can be understood without a deep understanding of the economic, social, and political conditions that shaped them.

In that sense, the Protestant International is both a cause and a consequence of the increasing globalization of the modern era in all its complexity.

In Conclusion, there are two points that need to be made with crystal clarity. The first is that I have organized my interpretation of the Protestant International around revitalization movements, which over time can become consolidated and sterile or else morph into something quite different. There are, of course, other ways a Protestant International could be constructed around Protestant denominations and their hierarchies or around the ideas of theological elites, but these are not so amenable to my structural framework of nuclei, nodes, and networks, and in any case much of this approach is already well documented. Second, my historical construction of a Protestant International is not intended to function as a normative argument for Christianity in general or evangelical Protestantism in particular as a uniquely universalizing religion and hence one that has a special mandate and ideological justification for global transmission. Much of the "international" highlighted in this chapter was produced and shaped by a specific set of historical contingencies, which played out in various parts of the world in complex ways. Claims of divine authorization by historical actors are not the same thing as divine authorization, however that is to be interpreted.

5

Women's Networks

Opportunities and Limitations

~

Organize, agitate, educate, must be our war cry

Susan B. Anthony (1820–1906)

This chapter is animated by an overarching question from which other questions naturally flow. What are the characteristics of the religious networks, nodes, and nuclei constructed by women and to what extent do they function differently from those built largely by men?[1] In attempting to answer that question, I will identify five different kinds of networks and look at some case studies within each category.[2] In practice, these networks may have overlapping characteristics, but are nevertheless sufficiently distinctive for purposes of analytical clarity.

---

[1] I am grateful to my colleague Ann Braude, Director of the Women's Studies in Religion Program at Harvard University, and to my doctoral student, Kelsey Hanson Woodruff, for their help in researching this lecture. For a helpful conceptual framing of the issues see Ann Braude, "Women's History Is American Religious History," in Thomas A. Tweed (ed.), *Retelling U.S. Religious History* (Berkeley, 1997), 87–107.

[2] I am deliberately not going over the same ground I covered on women's networks, such as the Woman's Christian Temperance Union, in my book, *Evangelical Disenchantment: Nine Portraits of Faith and Doubt* (New Haven, 2008), 92–113. That is not to diminish the importance of the women I wrote about then, including Sarah Grimké, Elizabeth Cady Stanton, and Frances Willard, or the issues they cared about, namely slavery, female suffrage, and temperance.

I should make clear at the start that the following questions and typology should not be read as either an *ascension* or *declension* narrative about women's agency and the role of patriarchy in shaping female agency. Saba Mahmood remains an influential voice in contending for "an analytical language for thinking about modalities of agency that exceed liberatory projects (feminist, leftist, or liberal)."[3] Women, either as individuals or in groups or networks, act within and upon political, ethical, and cultural contexts which they shape and are shaped by. Historians, sociologists, and other commentators may have pre-assigned sets of values that enable them to make judgments on the ethical validity of whatever agency is being exercised, but we should be careful not to delegitimize agency because we happen to disagree with the purposes for which it is exercised. Put another way, women within religious traditions, however patriarchal they appear to be, have discovered all kinds of ways of finding empowerment and fulfilment that may not fit neatly into progressive emancipatory paradigms. As my colleague Catherine Brekus, when writing about Mormon women, has concluded, female agency even in very conservative religious traditions takes place within structures as well as against them; is always shaped by cultural norms and constraints; operates within a

---

[3] Saba Mahmood, *Politics of Piety: The Islamic Revival and the Feminist Subject* (Princeton, 2012). This book was first published in 2005. The quote is from the Preface to the 2012 edition (page x) in which the author surveys the reaction to her ideas. See also Saba Mahmood, "Feminist Theory, Embodiment and the Docile Agent: Some Reflections of the Egyptian, Islamic Revival," *Cultural Anthropology*, 16, 2 (2001), 202–36.

continuum not a binary; is always marked by gender, racial, and class disparities; and does not have to be associated with freedom and emancipation or intentional or unintentional subversion of patriarchy.[4] One must also be careful not to exaggerate the role of female agency, both intentional and unintentional, in directly *causing* complex historical changes to which they may be significant contributors. Finally, however careful one is not to ideologically disqualify the role of female agency, especially in conservative religious traditions, it is good to be reminded of Ruth Bader Ginsburg's oft-quoted ethical imperative that "women belong in all the places that decisions are being made." That is demonstrably not the case in the patriarchal *hierarchies* of traditional religious institutions, which is why the study of female *networks* is of such vital importance.

So, to be clear, my task in this chapter is to bring to life women's transnational religious networks, nodes, and nuclei and to ask the question how they differ from those constructed by men, rather than to engage in a rigorous theoretical and practical evaluation of female agency itself. Here, then, are my five categories. The first are those networks that operate mostly within religious denominations or traditions as expressions of piety, fellowship, community, and mutual support. These networks, some of which were established by men at their very beginning, are generally not designed to challenge male hegemony directly or undermine

[4] Catherine Brekus, "Mormon Women and the Problem of Historical Agency," *Journal of Modern History*, 37, 2 (Spring 2011), 58–87. See also Jennifer Einspahr, "Structural Domination and Structural Freedom: A Feminist Perspective," *Feminist Review*, 94 (2010), 1–19.

religious traditions. There are multiple examples within mainstream denominations of all kinds and ethnic backgrounds, and still others, like Aglow International, which are trans-denominational, transnational, and are held together by a shared theology and vision. A second category of networks are those that were not established by women for a particular feminist purpose, but came either to be dominated by women or were utilized by women in ways that shaped their cultural outcomes and impacted the experiences of their female participants in major ways. Examples include the Protestant missionary societies and organizations like the Student Christian Movement, both of which opened up a wide range of transnational experiences for women. A third category are those transnational networks of women that enabled them to create nodes in which they got to call most of the shots, but in which they also had to operate within preexisting structures and spaces of maleness, colonialism, race, and economies. Examples include female Catholic religious orders, like the Ursulines, which established networks of spiritual economies throughout the world in the colonial era. A fourth category are those female networks that are created specifically to put pressure on male-dominated religious traditions to promote change and equality. These include the Catholic feminist movements formed by women to end or modify an all-male priesthood or to campaign for female reproductive rights. Finally, there are networks fashioned by women on the margins of religious traditions to promote solidarity and community in the face of patriarchal theologies, structures, and control mechanisms which women find unacceptable. Examples include female progressive movements within conservative religious traditions such as American evangelicalism and Mormonism. The fourth and fifth categories announced here often elide into one another. Women's networks sometimes start as attempts to pressurize male hierarchies to change their theologies and policies. Sometimes they meet with partial success and sometimes they fail. Even when their primary objective fails, however, many of these networks adapt by creating new spaces for women to thrive beyond the reach of male establishments, while still affirming their commitment to the faith traditions they want to change.

A good place to begin is with a confession of the soul. Although I had worked on Methodism as a popular religious movement for several decades, it took a long time for me to absorb the reality that Methodism, both demographically and functionally, was predominantly a female religious movement, as indeed are most Western religious traditions. In my defense, weak though I now know it to be, the animating questions confronting me as a young doctoral student and the preponderance of materials in Methodist archives all pointed to a different set of analytical categories around political culture, institution building, internecine squabbles, theological polemics, conflicts based on social class, and anti-Catholicism. Once the light was switched on that Methodism was a predominantly women's movement, a whole fresh set of analytical categories came into view. In *Methodism: Empire of the Spirit*, I wrote that "as purveyors of hospitality, deaconesses, visitors, evangelists, prayers, exhorters, testifiers, class members and leaders, and preachers," women defined the character of the

Methodist movement.[5] Extending further, some historians of Methodism focused their attention on female Methodist discourse revealing a greater preoccupation with physical pain, suffering, and the fragility of life occasioned by their own experiences of childbirth, infant mortality, primitive medicine, visitation of the sick and vulnerable, and the mutual support of other women. Women were also central to the generational transmission of faith to children and to the hospitality networks on which the whole movement depended for the maintenance of an itinerant ministry and an organization built around classes and small groups. Looked at this way, the nucleus of Methodism looks somewhat different from that imagined by predominantly male and, in terms of historical influence, predominantly Marxist or socialist historians.[6] Similarly, the networks of women, both informally in the day-to-day interactions of Methodist women and more formally through classes organized by gender and marital status, were far more pervasive and influential than historians recognized, at least before the 1980s.

---

[5] David Hempton, *Methodism: Empire of the Spirit* (New Haven, 2005), 138. See also Catherine A. Brekus, *Strangers and Pilgrims: Female Preaching in America, 1740–1845* (Chapel Hill, 1998); A. Gregory Schneider, *The Way of the Cross Leads Home: The Domestication of American Methodism* (Bloomington, IA, 1993); Jean Miller Schmidt, *Grace Sufficient: A History of Women in American Methodism, 1760–1939* (Nashville, 1999); Paul Wesley Chilcote (ed.), *Her Own Story: Autobiographical Portraits of Early Methodist Women* (Nashville, 2001); Cynthia Lynn Lyerly, *Methodism and the Southern Mind, 1770–1810* (New York, 1998); and Dee E. Andrews, *The Methodists and Revolutionary America: The Shaping of an Evangelical Culture* (Princeton, 2000).

[6] See Phyllis Mack, *Heart Religion in the British Enlightenment: Gender and Emotion in Early Methodism* (Cambridge, 2008).

What is true for Methodism largely holds for its daughter movement, Pentecostalism. As with Methodism, the majority of worldwide Pentecostals are women, roughly in the proportion of three to two or higher in some places. In some respects, gender roles are remarkably similar to those of Methodism in an earlier period. Hierarchical roles in Pentecostal traditions are held by men, though there has been a tradition of charismatically gifted female leaders and preachers in American and Global-South Pentecostal traditions.[7] David and Bernice Martin have drawn attention to the generative ambiguity of gender roles within Pentecostalism, which they state has often been "dismissed as old patriarchy revived, but that has to be set against 'the gender paradox' analyzed by so many researchers, and the fact that this is a woman's movement. In the accelerating mobilization of those not heard from before, the women are the movers and the shakers."[8] The "gender paradox" is understood to be the asymmetry between the hierarchical positions of leadership held by men on the one hand, and on the other the ways in which women have

[7] For a good survey of the role of women leaders in global Pentecostalism, see Allan Heaton Anderson, *To the Ends of the Earth: Pentecostalism and the Transformation of World Christianity* (New York, 2013), 93–117.

[8] David Martin, *Pentecostalism: The World Their Parish* (Oxford, 2002), 169. Bernice Martin, "The Pentecostal Gender Paradox: A Cautionary Tale for the Sociology of Religion," in Richard K. Fenn (ed), *The Blackwell Companion to the Sociology of Religion* (Oxford, 2003), 52–66. See also Elizabeth E. Brusco, *The Reformation of Machismo: Evangelical Conversion and Gender in Colombia* (Austin, 1995) and "Gender and Power," in Allan H. Anderson, Michael Bergunder, André Droogers, and Cornelis van der Laan (eds.), *Studying Global Pentecostalism: Theories and Methods* (Berkeley, 2010), 74–92.

been enabled to promote family disciplines and moral order in the domestic sphere against male machismo and libertinism.

A primarily women's organization arising out of Pentecostalism, Aglow International, formerly known as Women's Aglow Fellowship, was described in an important ethnographic study in the 1990s as the largest interdenominational women's organization in the United States and probably the world. Begun in 1967, Aglow had its origins in the charismatic movements of the 1960s and now, according to its website, "In over 170 nations, Aglow is mobilizing millions into a company of warriors, champions, and global leaders of significance. We provide vision, leader development and resources for 20,000 volunteer leaders worldwide – touching 17 million lives annually."[9] Aglow started initially as the women's version of the Full Gospel Men's Business Fellowship, and soon became a movement of women, for women, and by women. The organization now has what it calls "Men of Issachar" groups, which are named after a verse in the Hebrew Bible about men "who understood the times" (1 Chronicles 12:32). Aglow has identity, vision, and mission statements, a standard charismatic evangelical statement of faith emphasizing the baptism of the Holy Spirt and tongue-speaking, and is essentially a worldwide network of small groups of women meeting for prayer, Bible study, and social action. Its particular self-declared mandates are to promote gender reconciliation under biblical principles, to "minister" to Muslims, and to "stand in loving support of Israel and

---

[9] "Give," Aglow, www.aglow.org/give.

the Jewish people."[10] Under that broad umbrella, the social actions of local groups from country to country are mostly directed at local and culturally specific issues that directly affect the well-being of women and their communities, including sexual trafficking. Aglow is also an evangelistic organization with a commitment to reach the "unreached," with a special interest in making an impact on the geographical zones between the tenth and fortieth parallels, which are regions with strong Muslim concentrations.

Aglow International is a hierarchically organized, international network of small groups, called Lighthouses in the US and Candlelight groups in the rest of the world, with headquarters in Edmonds, Washington, and with a woman President, Jane Hansen Hoyt. In her ethnographic study of Aglow groups in New England, Marie Griffith draws attention to a somewhat different version of "the gender paradox" identified above, namely, "Conservative evangelical women who believe that their true liberation is found in voluntary submission to divine authority." She concludes that, for the women of Aglow, "Notions of submission and surrender, of secrecy, openness, and intimacy, and of healing and transformation – all of which are enacted through prayer, through stories, and through changed behavior in everyday life – provide these women with means of reinventing themselves, of 'making room' for new selves within a social context that is also believed to be made new."[11] Griffith's critical

[10] "Foundational Truths," Aglow International, https://tinyurl.com/4hydhk7f.
[11] R. Marie Griffith, *God's Daughters: Evangelical Women and the Power of Submission* (Berkeley, 1997), 199, 213.

empathy leaves room simultaneously for claims of female agency in constructing new lives of disciplined devotion and for feminist critiques that these new selves are largely fashioned within patriarchal constructions of authority and control exercised by men. The nucleus of Aglow is a gendered view of how "kingdom values" expand throughout the world, expressed in the phrase from its website that "men take mountains and women crush chaos."[12] With a woman president, a majority female board (nine of eleven), and a network sustained by sophisticated messaging, national and international conferences, and tight fellowships of women in small groups, Aglow has been around for more than half a century and shows no signs of decline.

Aglow is an example of a transnational interdenominational network organized specifically by women for women, but there are other transnational Christian networks that were not initially started by women, but within which women have exercised disproportionate influence. One important example are the Protestant missionary societies, which were initially started by men but, by the end of the nineteenth century, women's mission organizations, with their army of local auxiliaries, existed in nearly every Protestant denomination. In 1900, around 57 percent of American Protestant missionaries were women, a proportion that continued to increase in the early twentieth century. Moreover, "the presence of unmarried women along with missionary wives meant that missionary women outnumbered missionary men by nearly two

---

[12] "Dominion Prayer," Aglow, www.aglow.org/ministries/prayer/mtm-wcc.

to one in the major mission fields."[13] The implications of these statistics are enormous, not just for the lives of the women who sailed from America to foreign destinations in their tens of thousands, but also to understand better the character of twentieth-century American imperialism at home and abroad. This "global network of American Protestant women," through their impact on education, health care, social activism, and the lives of women and children, were both witting and unwitting agents of what has been termed a "soft imperialism," a gendered analysis of which "is essential if scholars are to explore how American empire is perceived, experienced, and negotiated around the world."[14]

The sheer scale of the impact of American and European missionaries on the rest of the world in the twentieth century is as impressive as it is hard to evaluate. The difficulty is caused not only by the relative lack of research on the extensive geographical networks of women missionaries from multiple denominational and independent traditions, but also by the geopolitical, theological, and sociocultural turbulence of the twentieth century. Disrupted by two world wars, fierce theological conflicts between liberals and fundamentalists, the demise of colonialism and the rise of nationalist movements, and persistent contests between female empowerment and male instruments of control, women frequently found themselves embroiled in mega changes which they could

---

[13] Dana L. Robert, *Gospel Bearers, Gender Barriers: Missionary Women in the Twentieth Century* (Maryknoll, NY, 2002), 5.

[14] Barbara Reeves-Ellington, Kathryn Kish Sklar, and Connie A. Shemo (eds.), *Competing Kingdoms: Women, Mission, Nation, and the American Protestant Empire, 1812–1960* (Durham, NC, 2010), 2.

not control and of which they were often victims. In the midst of this complexity, five points stand out.

The first is the persistent determination of women missionaries to bear witness to what they considered to be the truths of the Gospel and its liberationist possibilities, whether as representatives of women's missionary organizations, Holiness traditions, or faith-mission style evangelistic enterprises. American women missionaries, however sensitive they were to Indigenous cultural sensibilities, generally believed that "all people deserved the triple advantages of Protestant Christianity, American civilization, and American forms of government."[15] Inevitably, that triptych could carry with it an anti-Catholic, anti-Orthodox, and anti-non-Christian religions charge, a chauvinistic approach to local racial and cultural realities, and flag-waving potential that was often modified, if not eliminated, by female agency in meeting real human needs. Sometimes the most effective tools of influence were also the most subtle.

Second, there was an almost relentless determination by men, whether on mission boards, in denominational leadership, or in other structures of power, to establish bureaucratic control mechanisms to ensure that women missionaries stayed within the boundaries of what they deemed to be acceptable behavior. For example, in the interwar years, partly to get control of the money raised by women and partly as a result of theological changes within American Christianity, many American denominations eliminated their national, female mission organizations. According to Dana Robert, "ironically, a movement

---

[15] Reeves-Ellington et al., *Competing Kingdoms*, 4.

that had sought empowerment for Christian women around the world found itself disempowered by patriarchal forces within the Western churches themselves."[16] In the history of Christianity, she writes, "the charismatic leadership of women has often been supplanted by more formalized male leadership,"[17] and women's missions fit the pattern. The most controversial issue was invariably who controlled the money. Women raised it and men often wrested it from them for the purposes they deemed most essential.

The third point to emphasize is that Western women missionaries thought they were the beneficiaries and therefore the representatives of a Christian civilization, which for all its weaknesses had delivered to them education, skills, and freedom to choose their own paths. Hence, women both consciously and unconsciously transmitted aspects of Western civilization, including its cultural and theological shifts over the course of their lives, and filtered back experiences and perceived lessons from their chosen destinations. In that sense, understanding the transnational dimension to women's missions has to be geographically capacious, both within and without the United States.

Fourth, women seem to have been particularly influential Christian ambassadors, not only in the lives of other women and children in host cultures, but also in empowering Indigenous leaders, both men and women, because they were perceived not to be in such obvious competition for power and control of Indigenous churches in the way that male missionaries often were. There are

---

[16] Robert, *Gospel Bearers*, 10.   [17] Robert, *Gospel Bearers*, 15.

many examples of women helping to educate, train, and empower indigenous male leaders.[18] One reason why missionary women were able to educate and train Indigenous men had to do with racism against men of color and men in other cultures that were presumed not to be equal to Western men, who, unlike children, could not be taught by women.

Finally, as more of research on female missionaries is done and their full-orbed stories are told, the more complex is the resulting picture. "U.S. women's missionary work both fed and undermined empires, national states, and the free rein of capitalist markets."[19] Female missionaries reinforced both racism and exclusion, at home and abroad, but on occasions helped undermine it in service of a female internationalism. Women were always operating within constraints imposed by mission boards, political pressure, colonial realities, and Indigenous sensibilities. Mostly, they were neither fully independent actors nor unquestioning adherents to pre-assigned ideologies of race, nation, and gender. The dominant theme is the insistent ambiguity of women's experience and legacy.

The fast-paced globalization of Christianity in the last century has produced a situation where most world Christians live in the Global South and the majority of that majority are women. Although networks of Western women missionaries in the nineteenth and twentieth centuries did not produce those statistics singlehandedly,

[18] Robert, *Gospel Bearers*, especially chapters 2, 4, 5, and 6.
[19] Mary A. Renda, "Doing Everything: Religion, Race and Empire in the U.S. Protestant Women's Missionary Enterprise, 1812–1960," in Reeves-Ellington et al., *Competing Kingdoms*, 368–69.

there can be no doubt that they played a very significant role, not just in the bare demographics, but also in the characteristics of Indigenous Christian traditions that are now themselves the senders of missionaries.

One religious tradition that now finds itself in the crucible of the changes in global Christianity, and the participation of women in those changes, is the Church of Jesus Christ of Latter-day Saints. In 1996, for the first time, more Mormons lived outside the United States than inside.[20] This startling shift from the original mission strategy of Mormonism to gather its devotees to its central geographical node in Utah was accomplished by a wide range of factors.[21] They include centrally directed missions and dissemination via the growing networks of globalization, including trade routes, migration patterns, channels of information, and government service. Change and growth in global Mormonism was both vigorously orchestrated from the center and serendipitously generated from the peripheries.[22] Important to the story are

[20] It should be noted that members of the Church of Jesus Christ of Latter-day Saints affirm the full title of their church for themselves, but for economy of expression I am using the conventional, widely used label, "Mormon."

[21] See Christopher Blythe, *Terrible Revolution: Latter-Day Saints and the American Apocalypse* (New York, 2020); Reid L. Neilson and Fred E. Woods, *Go Ye Into All the World: The Growth and Development of Mormon Missionary Work* (Provo, UT, 2012); David Golding, "Gender and Missionary Work," in Taylor G. Petrey and Amy Hoyt (eds.), *The Routledge Handbook of Mormonism and Gender* (Milton, 2020).

[22] I am grateful to Emily Farnsworth for access to her unpublished research paper, "'We Are Not Resting on Our Oars:' The Evolution in Modes of Expansion of the Church of Jesus Christ of Latter-day Saints" (Harvard, 2020), which shows how many new sites of Mormon penetration in the Global South started not with missionaries, but with other factors. She concludes, "The underlying, overlapping,

three policy changes, one in 1898 adding women to the missionary ranks, the second in 1978 when the Church issued a statement effectively ending racially based restrictions to the priesthood, and the third in 2012 lowering the age requirement (to nineteen from twenty-one) for Mormon women missionaries, thereby increasing the pool of unmarried women. By 2016 there were some 75,000 Mormon missionaries, more than a quarter of whom were women; "no other religion – Christian or not – comes even close to maintaining this number of full-time missionaries."[23] For Mormon women missionaries, many of the same patterns play out as with women missionaries in other Christian traditions: opportunities for leadership and foreign travel; new skill sets and growing self-confidence; but also coping with demeaning stereotypes and male control mechanisms.

As with women missionaries, so with their female converts. Mormonism offers women in the Global South some of the same advantages as other fast-growing Christian traditions, such as Pentecostalism: clear moral boundaries and family stability, an ability to translate the communal orientation of village life to urban settings, and an acceptance of patriarchy in exchange for greater emotional and material security for women and children. "Where the Latter-day Saints depart from other Christian

and situationally specific geological deposits of political, economic, imperial, educational, and international networks that facilitated everything from the assignments of foreign government personnel to the shipment of used books have shaped where, how, and on whose terms the Latter-day Saint tradition has spread through the world."

[23] Colleen McDannell, *Sister Saints: Mormon Women Since the End of Polygamy* (New York, 2019), 141.

traditions," however, "is in the benefits that a wealthy global church can provide its members" in terms of language training, financial help, and a sense of belonging to "a global network of Mormonism."[24] McDannell writes, "The very lack of Mormon architectural or ritual diversity signaled that one belonged to an international organization, not simply a local one. The widespread reach of the church was seen as evidence of the truth of its message. A South African could go to church in Botswana with her American missionary companion and feel right at home."[25] Mormonism, more than most other religious traditions, exported its distinctive brand unapologetically, both confident in its truth claims and organizationally determined to bring the medium and the message into close harmony.

Aside from the Mormons, the heyday of Protestant women missionaries from the United States was in the century between the Civil War and the Second World War, but in the decades immediately after World War II another form of transnational Christian service opened up for thousands of young American women. The Student Christian Movement and its many connected organizations, such as the YWCA, the World Student Christian Federation, denominational campus ministries, and later the University Christian Movement, opened up new opportunities for leadership, international travel, and education in the causes of social justice at home and abroad.[26] Most of these organizations were

---

[24] McDannell, *Sister Saints*, 134.   [25] McDannell, *Sister Saints*, 152.
[26] One could include in this list British and US college-based parachurch organizations such as Campus Crusade for Christ and InterVarsity Christian Fellowship. Mostly these organizations did not have

not led by women, but most had influential women leaders and staffers. For young women in the 1950s, 1960s, and 1970s, especially the growing cohorts of college students, these organizations introduced them to the great social and political issues of the day, including racism, civil rights, colonialism, and anti-Vietnam war activism. In the words of one of them, these organizations "changed their world and their worldview. It took them out of the context in which they were raised and introduced them to radically different perspectives in other parts of the country and around the globe. It also opened them up to their own capacities."[27] The nucleus of this global student movement of women was a concept of Christian service that was not rooted in older paradigms of proselytism, conversionism, colonialism, and denominationalism. What shines through in the autobiographies of the women who have recorded their stories is a shared commitment to an expansive national and international vision of a world order that could be revolutionized by a compassionate and socially conscious ethic of service and transformation. The nodes that helped give expression to this vision were university campuses and huge national and international conferences such as the 1959 Eighteenth Ecumenical Student Conference at Athens, Ohio, attended by students from all over the world and addressed by Martin Luther King, Jr. Arising

progressive worldviews, but they did offer women leadership positions that were not available in congregations. They also had international partner organizations and huge international conferences.

[27] Sara M. Evans (ed.), *Journeys that Opened Up the World: Women, Student Christian Movements, and Social Justice, 1955–1975* (Piscataway, NJ, 2003), 1.

from that conference was the idea for a new form of service in the shape of Frontier Interns who would travel to strategic frontiers and share in the collective struggle for justice.[28]

The networks of national and international service opened up by these organizations transformed the lives of women and paved the way for future careers as campus ministers, university professors, ordained ministers, women's rights advocates, and leaders of social justice organizations. It is striking how many of these women started out in Methodist youth organizations, showing both the longevity of that tradition's associational and radical social roots and its practices of lay leadership.[29] It is also noteworthy how some of these women, whatever their religious traditions, had to conceal aspects of their lives, including sexual identity, even in the supposedly radical currents of the 1960s and 1970s. Finally, the women who came together to tell their stories in Sarah Evans' book *Journeys that Opened Up the World* capture the flavor of women's networks that are less amenable to prosaic historical reconstruction: "Our intersecting and overlapping stories brought gales of laughter, tears of remembrance, and gasps of surprise as we realized not only how much we had forgotten but how much we never

---

[28] Evans, *Journeys that Opened Up the World*, 6–7.

[29] For the influence of Methodism, see the autobiographical essays by Sara Evans, Charlotte Bunch, Jill Hultin, Elmira Nazombe, Ruth Harris, Sheila McCurdy, and Jeanne Audrey, Powers in Evans, *Journeys that Opened Up the World*. Hillary Clinton also pays tribute to the Methodist tradition in her own journey of growing awareness about issues of social justice affecting women. Gary Scott Smith, *Do All the Good You Can: How Faith Shaped Hillary Rodham Clinton's Politics* (Urbana, IL, 2023).

knew – each in her own niche."[30] For these women, cama-
raderie built community, and community built capacity,
sometimes not fully recognized until later in their lives.
A third category of transnational women's networks,
also motivated by mission, are those created by female
Catholic religious orders which have deep roots in
European societies long before the Reformation and
Counter-Reformation era.[31] What changed in the sixteenth century was the fact that some of these religious
orders expanded westward to the Americas alongside the
Iberian and French colonial empires. The women who
founded the oldest cloistered convent in South America,
Santa Clara in Cuzco, Peru, in 1558, and those from other
religious orders who followed them, not only carved out
sacred space for their prayers and rituals but also played
important roles in the construction of Spanish colonial
hegemony.[32] The three colonial convents of Cuzco, Santa
Clara (1558), Santa Catalina (1605), and Santa Teresa
(1673), were virtually little cities within the city and were
spatially and ritually organized around the intense spiritual disciplines prescribed by their orders. The nuns
and the subordinate lay sisters and various categories of
mestizos under their care organized the daily practices
of convent life around their sacred vows of poverty,
chastity, and obedience, but they were also subservient to

---

[30] Evans (ed), *Journeys that Opened Up the World*, 9.
[31] See the succinct summary of women's religious orders before the
Reformation by Emily Clark, *Masterless Mistresses: The New Orleans
Ursulines and the Development of a New World Society, 1727–1834*
(Chapel Hill, 2007), 7–33.
[32] Kathryn Burns, *Colonial Habits: Convents and the Spiritual Economy of
Cuzco, Peru* (Durham, NC, 1999).

the requirements of the patriarchal fathers of the Cuzco colonial economy.[33]

The nuns of Cuzco were not operating within some sort of detached spiritual islands of religious devotion, but were active agents in the local economy through their dowries, property ownership, lending practices, and produce. The "spiritual economies" of the convents became vital cogs in the wheels of the Andean colonial order. For a long time they were beneficiaries as well as servants of this colonial order, but a series of economic changes in the late eighteenth century and the rise of nationalist movements in the nineteenth century eroded their social salience and confined them ever more to the solitude of the cloisters. In this way the female religious orders of Cuzco and many other places in the Iberian empires expanded their nodes and networks through colonialism, had their autonomy and practices moderated by the patriarchal necessities of imperial control, and had their influence reduced by the forces of colonial resistance. The obvious conclusion from the Cuzco example is that networks constructed by the female Catholic orders through colonialism, however rigorously constructed around the spiritual rules of their respective orders, could never function outside the social structures and expectations created by colonial elites. What was given on one hand could be taken away by the other.

A similar pattern, but with different results, is evident in the experience of the Ursulines who arrived in New Orleans in 1727. The Ursulines built a formidable network of more than three hundred schools in

---

[33] Burns, *Colonial Habits*, 101–31.

seventeenth-century France and were an order devoted to the education of women and girls. What made the New Orleans experiment especially interesting is that the Ursulines arrived in Louisiana under the French empire from 1727 to 1767, then had to adapt to Spanish imperial control from 1767 to 1803, and then found themselves part of the new American Republic. Further complicating their role was the fact that they educated women and girls of European, Native American, and African descent and were both slaveholders and practitioners of racial integration in their elite boarding schools. When the United States purchased Louisiana in 1803, there were only two other convents in the nation, both in Maryland, but in the subsequent three decades ten other orders of religious women were established in a much greater geographical area. In her book *Masterless Mistresses*, Emily Clark suggests that these Catholic female religious communities threatened male Protestant political culture at the intersection of race and gender. They not only "challenged the ideal of domesticity on which it rested by providing women with an alternative to marriage. They also offered a model of female benevolence with institutions that were not only governed by women but operated by women who were themselves self-governing and self-supporting."[34] Moreover, they blurred conventional racial lines by educating girls and women of color and allowing them to perform a number of roles anathema to the racial segregation of the South. Clark's argument is that these challenges to white, male, Protestant control of the new Republic sometimes magnified the anti-Catholicism of

[34] Clark, *Masterless Mistresses*, 262.

the antebellum republic which contributed directly to some grim events such as the burning of the Ursuline convent in Charlestown, Massachusetts, in 1834.

A fourth category of women's networks which have come to the fore in the last half century are those constructed by women within hierarchical and patriarchal religious traditions either to press for changes in denominational polities and policies or to carve out space for women to define their own religious practices and priorities. Perhaps the best-known examples are the Catholic feminist movements that emerged between the 1960s and 1980s partly out of the optimism about church reform created by Vatican II and partly as a distinctively Catholic expression of feminism. Given that the Roman Catholic Church is often regarded as almost the epitome of hierarchy and patriarchy, it is easy to assume that the words "Catholic feminist" are an oxymoron, but in her book *Catholic and Feminist*, Mary Henold boldly states that the historical record of the 1960s and 1970s "provides more than ample evidence that Catholic feminists existed, that they articulated a strong connection between their faith and their feminist principles, that they formed organizations to forward feminist agendas, that such organizations were networked into a larger movement of Catholic feminism, and that this movement had connections with the much larger American feminist movement."[35] In other

---

[35] Mary J. Henold, *Catholic and Feminist: The Surprising History of the American Catholic Movement* (Chapel Hill, 2008), 3. See also Julie Byrne, *The Other Catholics: Remaking America's Largest Religion* (New York, 2016). I am also grateful to Cheyenne Boon for sharing her unpublished research paper, "Catholic Feminist Movements through the Lens of Network Theory" (Cambridge, MA, 2020).

words, the Catholic feminist movement refers to a network of empowered people who held a "dual integrated commitment to their Catholic faith and to the struggle for women's liberation."[36] This "movement" had many different dimensions, from women intellectuals, theologians, and writers to specific organizations campaigning for female ordination or reproductive choice, and also different strategies and tactics from attempts to pressurize the Church's leadership into concessions to constructing alternative forms of praxis within which women could take leadership. Generally speaking, Catholic feminists focused their early efforts on seeking dialogue with Church authorities, but ended up expanding Catholic identity beyond the parameters proscribed by church officials. For example, the Women's Ordination Movement, which arose out of a conference in Detroit in 1975 and sought direct dialogue with church officials after its second national meeting in Baltimore in 1979, failed to make an impact, resulting in a strategy shift away from "seeking dialogue with the hierarchy to an increased emphasis on establishing separate women's communities on the church's 'margins.'"[37] One iteration of this trend, the Roman Catholic Womanpriests (RCWP) movement focused on ordaining women to lead Catholic parishes without official sanction, while another, the Women-Church Convergence, bypassed priesthood

[36] Henold, *Catholic and Feminist*, 1.
[37] See Maureen Fiedler and Dolly Pomerlau, "The Women's Ordination Movement in the Roman Catholic Church," in Rosemary Skinner Keller and Rosemary Radford Ruether (eds.), *Encyclopedia of Women and Religion in North America*, Volume 2 (Bloomington, IA, 2006), 951–60.

altogether in favor of lay-led communities of faith meeting in homes, but still for recognizably Catholic worship and fellowship.[38] There are now large numbers of "Independent Catholics," both conservative and liberal, in the United States and other parts of the world who remain fiercely Catholic but are not connected to the papacy. "Many left-leaning independents not only ordain women, but also perform same-sex marriages, open communion to all, and allow multiple religious affiliations among other surprising things."[39]

This evolution of strategy and practice over the issue of women's ordination was played out in similar ways around the issues of abortion and contraception. The organization Catholics for a Free Choice (now Catholics for Choice) was established in 1973 to serve as the voice of Catholics who wanted abortion on demand to be safe, legal, and available.[40] It established significant international connections, but once again the Church hierarchy played theological hardball over the issue and prevailed, at least superficially. What these feminist movements have demonstrated, however, is that while the patriarchal Catholic hierarchy has proved to be remarkably resilient,

[38] Rosemary Radford Ruether, "Should Women Want Women Priests or Women-Church?" *Feminist Theology* 20, 1 (2011), 63–72.
[39] Byrne, *The Other Catholics*, 4. Space does not permit analysis of another quite different kind of international network of Catholic devotion, namely Marian apparitions and the shrines and pilgrimages associated with them. See Sandra L. Zimdars-Swartz, *Encountering Mary: Visions of Mary from La Salette to Medjugorje* (Princeton, 1991).
[40] Frances Kissling, "Women's Freedom and Reproductive Rights: The Core Fear of Patriarchy," in Keller and Ruether (eds.), *Encyclopedia of Women and Religion in North America*, 1099–110. See also Patricia Miller, *Good Catholics: The Battle over Abortion in the Catholic Church* (Berkeley, 2014).

women's movements have also been successful in creating new forms of Catholic identity beyond the direct
control of that hierarchy. To be sure, many women have
left the Church in protest at its intransigence, but many
others have renegotiated the terms of their commitment in ways that allow them to remain Catholics and
feminists. Moreover:

without making any major political gains, Catholic feminists
slowly, quietly assumed leadership roles as pastoral associates,
pastoral administrators, theologians, liturgists, directors of
religious education, and seminary instructors. As the numbers
of priestly vocations plummeted throughout the eighties and
nineties, Catholic women, feminist or not, took up the slack
and have helped shape the religious lives of countless Catholics
in parishes across the country.[41]

Henold prefers not to call this cafeteria Catholicism,
which allows Catholic women to pick and choose what
aspects of church teaching they fancy, but rather a "liber-
ated Catholicism" in which women understand that their
religious lives are not imprisoned by male, hierarchical
power structures which they cannot yet change but which
do not define them.

As with Catholic feminists, so too with some other
religious traditions with male hierarchies, including the Mormons. Colleen McDannell shows how
Mormon feminists have used the internet, publications,
and occasionally direct action to protest Church policies on LGBTQ issues, the all-male priesthood, and
ultra-domesticated portrayals of the ideal Mormon

---

[41] Henold, *Catholic and Feminist*, 243.

homemaker and family. On the whole, they have met with the same fate as Catholic feminists and for some of the same reasons. The priesthood is still male, the hierarchy has not budged on issues stated to be essential to Mormon doctrine and practice, and women thought to be too extreme have been excommunicated. On the other hand, leaders have had to adapt to new realities by authorizing less sanitized versions of the Church's history (a double-edged sword) and to be somewhat more accommodating to LGBTQ issues without diminishing their commitment to the supposed divine endorsement of heterosexual marriage. Moreover, women continue to use digital media and women's organizations to evade the disciplinary structures of an authoritarian church. This uneasy tension between what the male hierarchy is willing to tolerate and what Mormon feminists want is not going to go away and may be exacerbated by the growing globalization of Mormonism. As McDannell puts it, the traditional domestic lifestyle blogging "presents a perfect home life that excludes almost everyone – single women as well as queer women, but also non-American members, Mormons of color, poor women, and almost every married woman who has an ordinary disorganized household."[42] The days are changing and conservative religious traditions of all hues are having to renegotiate their ideals and boundaries.

Evangelical Protestantism has a less centralized and hierarchical leadership structure than either Roman Catholicism or Mormonism, but its patriarchal credentials, at least in the United States, yield nothing to these

---

[42] McDannell, *Sister Saints*, 193.

other traditions. In her recent book, *Jesus and John Wayne*, Kristin Kobes Du Mez assembles a great deal of evidence to show that white evangelicals voted for Donald Trump in the 2016 election not "despite their beliefs, but because of them." She writes, "Evangelical support for Trump was no aberration, nor was it merely a pragmatic choice. It was, rather the culmination of evangelicals' embrace of militant masculinity, an ideology that enshrines patriarchal authority and condones the callous display of power, at home and abroad."[43] This bold and well-supported assertion is not without foundation, but possibly underestimates the myriad other factors around race, class, and social location that contribute to voting behavior. Others have drawn attention to the precarious place occupied by evangelical women celebrities as wives, preachers, and writers as they negotiate between the fine lines of influence and expectation. According to Kate Bowler, these women "must be pretty, but not immodest, exemplary, but not fake, vulnerable to sin, but not deviant."[44]

Of course, there is another tradition within evangelicalism, both of strong independent women who exercised considerable influence within the tradition in Britain and America and more generally of women who exercised leadership roles in times of novelty and

[43] Kristin Kobes Du Mez, *Jesus and John Wayne: How White Evangelicals Corrupted a Faith and Fractured a Nation* (New York, 2020), 3. It should be noted that voting behavior is notoriously difficult to account for. Religion is often a re-enforcing variable, but rarely an independent variable outside regional location, educational background, and social class.
[44] Kate Bowler, *The Preacher's Wife: The Precarious Power of Evangelical Women Celebrities* (Princeton, 2019). Quote taken from the dust jacket.

expansion before men re-established control.[45] In more recent times, there has been a paucity of treatment of those women who were decidedly not Trump supporters – the politically progressive women at the margins of evangelicalism.[46] These women, both white and women of color, have used digital media, publishing networks, and conference gatherings to build "robust communities" and "female-dominated counter-publics" to contest the dominant male evangelical narrative, particularly around LGBTQ and social justice issues.[47] Some of these women will join the ranks of disenchanted evangelicals and eventually find their way out of the evangelical tradition, but many others are using the tools at their disposal – digital, print, and conference – to construct and disseminate an alternative evangelical narrative around gender, race, and political praxis.

The situation is yet more complex for women in Black American religious denominations and traditions. On the one hand, research and writing about women in these traditions historically pay tribute both to the importance of the Black church and to the contribution of women's organizational networks within the church "to broadening the public arm of the church and making it the most powerful institution of racial self-help in the African

---

[45] See, for example, Brekus, Strangers & Pilgrims; Catherine A. Brekus, *Sarah Osborn's World: The Rise of Evangelical Christianity in Early America* (New Haven, 2013); Boyd Stanley Schlenther, *Queen of the Methodists: The Countess of Huntingdon and the Eighteenth-Century Crisis of Faith and Society* (Durham, UK, 1997).

[46] This is the subject of a Harvard PhD thesis currently in progress by Kelsey Hanson Woodruff. I am grateful to her for allowing me access to her dissertation prospectus.

[47] Woodruff, PhD thesis.

American Community."[48] Evelyn Brooks Higginbotham has brilliantly shown how the women's movement within the Black Baptist Church, organized through the formation of the Woman's Convention in 1900, advocated for values of self-help respectability (the politics of respectability) "both as a goal in itself and as a strategy for reform of American race relations."[49] The seven-point manifesto adopted by the Women's Convention in 1913, entitled "What We Want and What We Must Have," "drew upon the politics of respectability in a demand for broad structural changes in society to reform the South's educational, electoral, judicial, and penal systems."[50] These Black women invested in personal uplift, community solidarity, and large-scale civic reform. Women's negotiation for recognition and power within their churches and their communities, often perceived as a challenge to conventional patriarchal theology, could also be a source of tension. In Anthea Butler's words, "Women's authority to own their own sacred space and men's fears of women taking their pastoral authority have driven much of the organizational and strategic infighting in churches."[51] These tensions articulated by historians of Black churches in the nineteenth and early twentieth centuries have not gone away. A more recent study based

[48] Evelyn Brooks Higginbotham, *Righteous Discontent: The Women's Movement in the Black Baptist Church, 1880–1920* (Cambridge, MA, 1993), 1. See also Judith Weisenfeld, *African American Women and Christian Activism: New York's Black YMCA, 1905–1945* (Cambridge, MA, 1998).
[49] Higginbotham, *Righteous Discontent*, 187.
[50] Higginbotham, *Righteous Discontent*, 222.
[51] Anthea Butler, *Women in the Church of God in Christ: Making a Sanctified World* (Chapel Hill, 2007), 6.

on a national sample of 1,863 Black churches across seven denominations found that, especially among Baptists and Pentecostals, opposition to racial injustices mostly take precedence over issues of gender disparity within church hierarchies, including support for women pastors.[52] Other big data surveys suggest that church networks are particularly important for African American women (and men for that matter) and may have positive benefits in terms of emotional and material support, and physical and mental health.[53] What these various historical accounts and survey data show is that although one needs to calibrate carefully by denomination, social class, marital status, and geographical location, church networks are vitally important for African American women and that they can advance social justice and racial self-help without necessarily promoting gender equity.[54] Here again, times are changing both nationally and internationally as the World Council of Churches now organizes a Pan African Women's ecumenical Empowerment Network to develop leadership capacity and theological education for women of African descent throughout the world.

This chapter began with the question of whether or not the nuclei, nodes, and networks constructed by women operate differently from those built by men. That opened

---

[52] Sandra L. Barnes, "Whosover Will Let *Her* Come: Social Activism and Gender in the Black Church," *Journal for the Scientific Study of Religion*, 45, 3 (2006), 371–87.

[53] Ann W. Nguyen, Robert Joseph Taylor, Linda M. Chatters, and Meredith O. Hope, "Church Support Networks of African Americans: The Impact of Gender and Religious Involvement," *Journal of Community Psychology*, 47, 5 (2019), 1043–63.

[54] See Henry Louis Gates, Jr., *The Black Church: This Is Our Story, This Is Our Song* (New York, 2021).

up five subsidiary questions about the role of women's networks in the transmission of religious belief and practice over some five hundred years. Three important themes have emerged. The first is that most religious traditions and movements have majorities of women, but most are led by men and are based on deeply embedded patriarchal assumptions. That underlying reality is played out in multiple different Christian traditions and shapes the subsequent contests for power, representation, and influence. A second theme is that women have found imaginative ways to create spheres of influence within, and sometimes even to control, the religious traditions they inhabit. That influence has to be mediated, not only by the structures of male power within religious traditions, but also by the structures of male power operating in the political, economic, social, and cultural arrangements of the wider society. For example, however much female religious orders in the early modern period kept control of their own institutions, they were always embedded in colonial structures and local economies which were normally beyond their control.

Finally, women's networks often serve contrasting functions from those built by men, who begin with the luxury of centuries-old foundations of ideological/theological power and who are also able to utilize the transmission agencies built by other men. In light of these disadvantages and discriminations, women, in common with other marginalized communities, often experience both the joys and disappointments of their nodes and networks in more acute ways than the men who set the rules and conditions. In that sense, womanhood itself is at the heart of the religious nucleus that bound together the

Christian sisterhoods of women's networks as their shared sets of experiences and values gave rise to a distinctive female consciousness, whatever the specific circumstances that called any given network into existence.[55] Perhaps more than anything, that is the secret of their enduring strength and influence.

[55] See Nancy Cott, *Bonds of Womanhood: "Woman's Sphere" in New England, 1780–1835* (New Haven, 1977).

6

"Only Connect!"

Christianity in the Digital Age

~

E. M. Forster's novel, *Howard's End*, with its oft-quoted epigraph "Only Connect" (the prose and the passion), about the developing connections between the Schlegel and Wilcox families, respectively the worlds of personal relationships, arts, and culture, and the worlds of business, capitalism, and pragmatism, anticipates by more than a century some of the important questions about the impact of revolutionary changes in global connectivity in the age of the internet and its consequences for the history of Christianity. We started this book with some reflections from Niall Ferguson's *The Square and the Tower*, which he bookends with two revolutions: print in the sixteenth century and the internet and social media in the late twentieth century. "The global impact of the internet," he writes, "has few analogues in history better than the impact of printing on sixteenth-century Europe. The personal computer and smartphone have empowered networks as much as the pamphlet and the book did in Luther's time."[1] He also notes some major differences. First, the networking revolution has been faster and more geographically extensive; second, it has increased inequality and concentrated fabulous wealth in fewer hands; and

---

[1] Niall Ferguson, *The Square and the Tower: Networks and Power, from the Freemasons to Facebook* (New York, 2018), 400.

third, the printing press disrupted religious life before
anything else, whereas the internet disrupted commerce
first, and in Ferguson's opinion has disrupted only one
religion: Islam.

Ferguson justifies this assertion by references to the
jihadist networks constructed by Islamic extremists, but
it is clearly not the case that Christianity has escaped
impact from the internet revolution; the question is
how, and, more broadly, how is Christianity changing
in the age of social media and international connectivity? Attempting answers to these questions is more complicated than assessing the impact of print on religious
change in the sixteenth century, at least in part because
we are currently living through the digital media revolution and we do not yet have the benefit of perspective and
accumulated research. Moreover, as influential recent
books have shown, we are only beginning to evaluate
and absorb the consequences of digital media on mental health and social connections.[2] While acknowledging
those realities, the aim of this chapter is to begin answer-
ing these questions by posing three subsidiary questions:
What social and cultural changes were already underway
in the decades immediately preceding the internet revolution which have a direct bearing on the generations
most affected by that revolution? What does the preliminary evidence reveal about the impact of new technologies and social media on the beliefs, practices, and "lived
religion" of Christian communities, organizations, and

[2] For example, Jonathan Haidt, *The Anxious Generation: How the Great
Rewiring of Childhood Is Causing an Epidemic of Mental Illness* (New York,
2024).

denominations? Finally, to what extent has the internet helped develop global religious networks in which the directional flows of power and influence have begun to change from a North to South trajectory to a South to North one?

Any answer to the first question has first to grapple with a vast and growing literature on secularization across the Western world, especially in the widely acknowledged key decade of the 1960s.[3] In a recent survey of that literature, Hugh McLeod states, "Historians and sociologists agree that the major changes in most Western countries included a decline in churchgoing and in participation in rites of passage; a weakening of religious socialisation; questioning of official church teaching, especially on sexual ethics; and an increasing tendency to see society as 'pluralist', or even 'secular', rather than 'Christian'."[4] This consensus, such as it is, does not extend to explanations for how, why, and at what speed this secularization, or perhaps more accurately, dechristianization, has happened from region to region and from country to country. Among the most persuasive are declining rates of generational transmission (partly as a result of greater female emancipation and participation in the workforce), the increasing role of the state in providing services previously offered by religious organizations, the primary secularization of young working-class men, the erosion of rural pockets of strong religiosity under pressure from modernizing trends, and the role of churches themselves

---

[3] See especially Hugh McLeod, *The Religious Crisis of the 1960s* (Oxford, 2007).

[4] Hugh McLeod, "Western Religion in the Long 1960s," *Journal of Ecclesiastical History*, 70, 4 (2019), 823–31.

through contributing to their own demise by liberalizing their theologies and participating in cultural changes that undermined their own claims for attention.[5] McLeod and I have tried to grapple with the comparative transatlantic dimensions of secularization in another book, but for present purposes, it is less important to agree on the how and why of secularization than on the rough consensus about what McLeod laid out in his review article and in another suggestive essay entitled "The Register, the Ticket and the Website."[6] Together they assert that several decades before the onset of the internet revolution and the proliferation of social media, the complex of cultural changes we associate with the long 1960s had already undermined generational transmission of faith traditions, promoted concepts of individual freedom from traditional authorities, including churches, and encouraged younger cohorts to construct their identities not through family inheritance or membership of local faith communities, but by self-actualizing individual choices freely made. All of these changes have

[5] See Callum G. Brown, *The Death of Christian Britain* (London, 2001); Hugh McLeod and Werner Ustorf (eds.), *The Decline of Christendom in Western Europe, 1750–2000* (Cambridge, 2003); Callum G. Brown and Michael Snape (eds.), *Secularisation in the Christian World* (Farnham, Surrey, 2010); Robert D. Putnam and David E. Campbell, *American Grace: How Religion Divides and Unites Us* (New York, 2010); Clive D. Field, *Secularization in the Long 1960s: Numerating Religion in Britain* (Oxford, 2017); and Sam Brewitt-Taylor, *Christian Radicalism in the Church of England and the Invention of the British Sixties, 1957–1970: The Hope of a World Transformed* (Oxford, 2018).
[6] David Hempton and Hugh McLeod (eds.), *Secularization and Religious Innovation in the North Atlantic World* (Oxford, 2017). Hugh McLeod, Unpublished Conference Paper presented to the conference on "Master Narratives of Religious Change," Amsterdam, April 2002.

been arguably reinforced and accelerated by the information revolution of the past thirty years.

There is already a formidable literature in existence about how the internet has impacted social norms or how religious traditions both exploit and suffer from digital technologies, or about the challenges of negotiating faith and theology under new conditions.[7] Some suggest that the internet and mobile technologies have effectively created a new social operating system labeled "networked individualism," at the center of which are autonomous individuals reaching out and interacting with others in multiple different social circles in fast-moving and complex patterns. This social system encourages fragmented networks of multiple social circles rather than deep investment in any particular community or congregation based on a pre-assigned affiliation of some. This is analogous to the concept of differentiation in secularization theory.[8] It is easy to see how this more fragmented structure managed by autonomous individuals, rather than by inherited familial or community faith traditions, effectively accelerates the changes already operating in post 1960s Western culture identified by scholars of secularization.

The fast-growing body of work on the impact of digital technologies on Christianity has identified four areas worthy of further analysis. The first relates to individuals and their search for online community, the second

---

[7] See Heidi Campbell, *Exploring Religious Community Online: We Are One in the Network* (New York, 2005) and Heidi A. Campbell and Stephen Garner, *Networked Theology: Negotiating Faith in Digital Culture* (Grand Rapids, MI, 2016).
[8] Campbell and Garner, *Networked Theology*, 8–9.

relates to how well religious institutions are adapting or not adapting to new informational technologies, the third focuses on challenges to traditional sources of authority and control, and the fourth relates to overall cultural assessments about how this communications revolution is altering the way in which Christian faith traditions function or do not function in the twenty-first century. Unsurprisingly, there are vigorous disagreements within each of these categories.

In her in-depth analysis of three quite different kinds of online religious communities, the Community of Prophecy, the Online Church, and the Anglican Communion Online, Heidi Campbell identified six attributes of online community that individuals were searching for: relationship, care, value, connection, intimate communication, and shared faith.[9] These are not substantially different from the attributes most desired from offline religious communities, but the online version confers more individual control, fewer geographical or temporal limitations, and more scope for individual spiritual experimentation and self-actualization. Moreover, many of those engaged with online religious communities saw them as supplemental rather than as necessarily binary alternatives to local faith communities. Religion online serves a variety of distinct functions, from a worship space to a prayer network, and from a support or identity network to a study or service portal. Equally variegated were the positive and negative poles of digital communication which could promote deep friendship and spiritual connection on the one hand, and spamming, flaming, stalking,

---

[9] Campbell, *Exploring Religious Community Online*, 195.

and inappropriate counselling and power maneuvers on the other. Most offline religious communities have structures of governance and mechanisms for exercising discipline, while most online communities are more unregulated and more vulnerable to rogue or destructive actors. Individuals certainly have a wider range of online choices available to them, both locally and globally, but the data suggest that, far from producing a more engaged transnational and interfaith pluralism, digital technologies may in fact reinforce a form of selective tribalism as online searchers gravitate to what most interests them. Ironically, the capaciousness of the web can easily result in the narrowness of the sect or the site.

A similar ambiguity about the pros and cons of online faith attachments for individuals is also the case for religious institutions. The survey data indicate that church leaders have steadily embraced blogs, podcasts, and social media as adjunct tools in their various ministries. Having said that, some traditions seem to have adapted better than others. Figures from the Billy Graham Evangelistic Association and Global Media Outreach show that conversionism plays well on the internet, while traditions more oriented around ritual and community find it harder to adapt.[10] For example, Campbell opens her latest book with a story about an application developed by an American software company to help Catholic penitents prepare for the sacrament of confession. This app had the blessing of some American Catholic leaders but caught the attention of the Vatican, which ruled that although the app was acceptable as a preparatory

---

[10] Campbell and Garner, *Networked Theology*, 1–3.

guide, it could not be a substitute for the embodied act of confession conducted by a priest.[11] In fact, the Vatican has been remarkably proactive in engaging with digital media. The Roman Catholic Church was the first religious denomination to launch its own website in 1996; it launched its own YouTube channel in 2009 and has employed Twitter, Facebook, and its own online news portal to get across its message. As churches and religious communities have sought to maximize social media, they have encountered new issues of authority and control. In particular, Campbell has shown that a new category of leaders, whom she calls Religious Digital Creatives, has emerged. Whether digital entrepreneurs using advanced algorithmic skills, digital spokespersons charged with effectively communicating a church's mission, or digital strategists negotiating online and offline authority structures within religious institutions, there is no denying that a powerful new group of specialists has emerged whose authority is based more on their digital expertise than their pastoral or theological credentials.[12] How that authority is exercised and under what constraints varies from congregation to congregation and, crucially, with the size of the religious enterprises. Unforeseen events such as the Covid-19 pandemic and the jet propulsion of Zoom gatherings further reinforced the dependence of churches and faith communities on the expertise of tech specialists. Faith communities, as with other kinds of institutions responsible for transmitting knowledge

---

[11] Heidi A. Campbell, *Digital Creatives and the Rethinking of Religious Authority* (New York, 2021), 1–4.

[12] See the excellent conclusion in Campbell, *Digital Creatives*, 193–209.

and information, will have to reckon with both the short-term and the long-term impact of the pandemic on the delivery of their mission. Virtual events often have much higher numbers of registrants but cannot reproduce the in-person convivialities of fellowship. It is also important to recognize that trends that seem to be unidirectional and inevitable may not turn out to be so. For example, a decade ago it seemed that the trend towards ebooks overtaking physical books with the consequent decline of real bookstores was irreversible, but more recent data indicate that most people still like browsing in book-stores and reading from material books. It remains to be seen whether digital forms of religious community will inexorably erode in-person gatherings or set up a counter reaction.

None of the three questions posed earlier about the impact of digital media on faith communities has unam-biguous answers, but perhaps the most difficult of all is the question about the overall cultural impact of social media on how churches function or do not function in these early decades of the twenty-first century. My main argument is that there is something of a conti-nuity between religious dimensions of the cultural and social changes of the long 1960s and the impact of social media over the past three decades, which have accelerated those changes.[13] Sometimes new networks are superim-posed on preexisting networks and derive their impetus from them. For example, Daniel Vaca's investigation of

[13] See, for example, Wade Clark Roof, *Spiritual Marketplace: Baby Boomers and the Remaking of American Religion* (Princeton, 1999), which is an insightful interpretation of trends in American religion c.1990s before the impact of the digital revolution.

evangelicalism as a "commercial religion" shows how the huge industry of religious book publishing and consumption, adapted to new realities when brick and mortar bookstores were forced to close under pressure from new digital dynamics. "If bookstores typified the old evangelical economy," writes Vaca, "the internet has been the heart of the new economy," enabling bestselling authors like the Californian pastor, Rick Warren, "to engage their publics more directly than before, cultivating their personal brands." Warren was able to generate a network of more than six thousand churches from eighty denominations in twelve countries, which enabled his publisher to sell fourteen million copies of his book in just a few years.[14] Others have suggested that the growth of new media, especially within younger cohorts, has eroded the Christian Right's political ascendancy within American evangelicalism with new emphases on climate change, protection of the environment, social and economic justice, and gay rights. With pardonable exaggeration, one recent study concludes, "The internet has completely redrawn the global landscape within the space of a generation, creating a much more interconnected world and fostering virtual communities where online users are able to engage in debate and faith exploration, freely exchange ideas, and even form new organizations, interest groups, and religious communities."[15] But there is also a darker side to these developments. A recent article in

[14] Daniel Vaca, *Evangelicals Incorporated: Books and the Business of Religion in America* (Cambridge, MA, 2019), 232.
[15] Christopher W. Boerl and Katie Donbavand, *A God More Powerful than Yours: American Evangelicals, Politics, and the Internet Age* (Newcastle upon Tyne, 2015), 110.

The New York Times, "Christian Prophecy Movement is hit hard by Trump's Defeat," states that social media have facilitated a bogus prophecy industry within American populist evangelicalism that is full of failed predictions about the results of the 2020 presidential election and sheering off into dangerous conspiracy theories such as those articulated by QAnon.[16]

If the digital age is opening up new possibilities for longstanding religious traditions like Roman Catholicism and evangelical Protestantism, it is also facilitating new forms of "spiritual-but-not-religious" expressions among those who have come of age in the internet era. Aware that millennials are less religiously affiliated than previous generations and that various American surveys of religiosity have identified the "nones," or religiously unaffiliated, as the fastest-growing category in the American religious landscape, two Harvard Divinity School students recently set out to interrogate these categories. What they discovered is that "millennials are flocking to a host of new organizations that deepen community in ways that are powerful, surprising, and perhaps even religious." They looked at ten of these organizations, from fitness clubs to social transformation organizations, and discovered that they had six things in common: community (valuing and fostering deep relationships that center on service to others); personal transformation (making a conscious and dedicated effort to develop one's own body, mind, and spirit); social transformation (pursuing justice and beauty in the world through the creation of networks for good); purpose finding (clarifying, articulating,

---

[16] *The New York Times*, February 12, 2021.

and acting on one's personal mission in life); creativity (allowing time and space to activate the imagination and engage in play); and accountability (holding oneself and others responsible for working toward defined goals). Unsurprisingly, they concluded that the organizations they surveyed "serve disproportionately affluent, urban, educated, and white populations," perhaps those populations that are vacating the Protestant mainline and more traditional Catholic congregations at the fastest rates.[17] Nevertheless, their most obvious conclusion is that many of the functions supplied by these organizations mirror quite closely, albeit with different descriptive language, those traditionally associated with religious congregations, thereby reinforcing their intuition that the category of "spiritual but not religious" is one that has particular appeal to younger generations of urban Americans.

A second example comes from a network constructed by one of the above investigators. Beginning with a week-long set of movie evenings based on the Harry Potter films, he and a friend effectively built up a "mini congregation" before launching "Harry Potter and the Sacred Text" as a podcast which now has more than twenty-two million downloads and seventy thousand weekly listeners. Based on techniques of disciplined sacred reading, this virtual community helps people connect with themselves, with others, and with issues in the wider world. Just how deep and meaningful these personal connections become is illustrated in some of the personal correspondence reproduced in a recent book on the power of ritual which

[17] Angie Thurston and Casper ter Kuile, *How We Gather* (pamphlet with no place and date of publication).

190

aims to reapply ancient wisdom on the importance of ritual to everyday practices.[18] Once again, wisdom traditions rooted in religious traditions are transmitted in modern idioms through networks enabled by digital media. This is networked individualism in action. This conclusion fits into a pattern of sociological research on the inter-relationship of religion and media based on extensive interviews across different religious and social categories. One such study concludes:

Our interviewees live in a post-Enlightenment, secularized (using a conditional definition of that term, of course), late-modern world, defined by personal autonomy, the self, and rational and reflexive modes of cultural practice. At the same time, though, they can be said to be involved in a process of "re-naturing" the religiosity or spirituality of these practices, building religion and spirituality into things through their rediscovered interest in invigorating social and cultural experience with these dimensions.[19]

This does not normally constitute a re-enchantment of the world into mystical religious categories, but it does not bode well for traditional religious authorities whose "pulpits" are de-centered by the democratization of mass media. On the other hand, some cultural analysts have identified a connection between cyberspace, immateriality, and spirituality. In these accounts, the digital domain, because of its evident immateriality, carries with it the possibility of "religious valorization" or of re-imagining "sacred space" because it is separate from

---

[18] Casper ter Kuile, *The Power of Ritual: Turning Everyday Activities into Soulful Practices* (New York, 2020).

[19] Stewart M. Hoover, *Religion in the Media Age* (New York, 2006), 289.

the physical realm and can be the subject of millenarian and spiritual fantasies.[20]

What then happens, to use a recent book title, when religion meets new media?[21] The answer, it seems, is predictably ambiguous. On the one hand, new media offer mechanisms and opportunities for more extensive proclamation of core beliefs, national and global networking, and community building via shared online rituals, while on the other hand they may expose the faithful to inappropriate content, weaken traditional authority structures, and place more power in the hands of dedicated and tech-savvy individuals with an agenda. One recent study of networked Christianity in the United States makes a much bolder claim that the future of Christianity in the United States and beyond is being changed forever. Locating their study of Independent Network Charismatic (INC) Christianity within the context of large-scale social changes, including globalization, the digital revolution, and the challenge to religious bureaucracies, Christerson and Flory argue that traditional denominational Christianity is in terminal decline in the United States. The future belongs to networks of independent churches that emphasize direct supernatural engagement, innovative financial and marketing strategies, and new digital communications technologies. Paralleling similar changes in the organization of global capitalism, INC leaders have realized that they have "more freedom, flexibility, and lower overhead by organizing

---

[20] See Margaret Wertheim, *The Pearly Gates of Cyberspace: A History of Space from Dante to the Internet* (New York, 1999), 256.
[21] Heidi A. Campbell, *When Religion Meets New Media* (London, 2010).

themselves into networks rather than by building formal organizations. They can maximize their influence and minimize their costs by going directly to the 'consumer' with their 'product' rather than delivering the product through a formal congregation or denomination."[22] Organized around networks of charismatic apostles, INC churches have significant competitive advantages over denominational Christianity in terms of the freedom to experiment and the raising of revenue. Instead of relying on the notoriously ineffectual plate collections and voluntary donations from congregants, INC churches raise the bulk of their income from web-based media sales (music, DVDs, books, web content), tuition, conferences, external donations, and monetizing their property assets. They also reduce expenditure on items that conventional churches must fund to build and sustain congregations, such as staffing, program management, property maintenance, and so on. In essence, "the typical congregation is a high overhead, low-revenue stream model," while the INC churches "have shifted towards a 'pay for service' model in which followers pay for a particular product."[23] As any business major will tell you, this model expands the customer base, refines the product, and generates a lot more money. All of this is facilitated by the internet which acts as a delivery platform, an advertising medium, a pay-per-view revenue stream, a virtual community of believers, and communication flows "not just from follower to leader and back. But horizontally among nodes

---

[22] Brad Christerson and Richard Flory, *The Rise of Network Christianity: How Independent Leaders are Changing the Religious Landscape* (New York, 2017), 45.
[23] Christerson and Flory, *The Rise of Network Christianity*, 121.

in the network."[24] However, not everything is rosy in the INC garden. Failed prophecies, lack of deep in-person community, financial and leadership scandals, and lack of a compelling overall social vision have all surfaced in the INC world, which is dominated by predominantly male prophets.

Whatever is in store for INC churches, Christerson and Flory propose four hypotheses about the future of Christianity itself based on their observations of INC networks: Religious belief and practice will become increasingly experiential; religious authority will devolve more to individuals than institutions; religion will become more orientated to practice than theology; and individuals will increasingly customize their own beliefs and practices.[25] Time will tell if these changes are inexorable, but there is no doubt that they are currently happening.

To recap, the argument presented so far in this chapter is that the profound social and cultural changes of the 1960s and 1970s which historians and sociologists have analyzed within the framework of secularization and differentiation were accelerated and redirected by the digital revolution and globalization. I have looked at the impact of new social media on religious belief and practice and on religious institutions. The four main conclusions arrived at by Christerson and Flory, though directly applicable to the INC churches in the United States at the center of their investigation, have wider salience for the future of Christianity, not only in the US, but around the world. Consequently, these changes also need to be placed in

[24] Christerson and Flory, *The Rise of Network Christianity*, 124.
[25] Christerson and Flory, *The Rise of Network Christianity*, 165–66.

the context of a dramatic shift in the distribution of world Christianity.

According to some estimates, some 60 percent of the roughly two billion Christians in the world are now located in the Global South (Latin America, Africa, and Asia), a figure that on current projections may rise to 75 percent of around three billion Christians by 2050. But the shift is not in numbers alone. In a recent book entitled *A Moving Faith: Mega Churches Go South* (2015), the writers attempt to identify common themes over a wide global geography.[26] These include the adaptability of charismatic/Pentecostal supernaturalism to Indigenous cultures; the transmission through networks of common tropes such as prosperity, healing, and material merchandizing of religious products; the marketing, branding and mediatization of faith; the attention to producing seeker-friendly, spatial environments for younger cohorts; a greater, if still limited, empowerment of women; and a growing interest in influencing wider social and political reforms. What is striking about these developments is how transnationally *networked* they are, promoted by the well-known instruments of globalization.

In a study of one particular nucleus at the center of many of these changes, the prosperity gospel, Kate Bowler writes that "the development of digital media only accelerated the breathtaking pace of transnational communication. The prosperity gospel was obsessed with modernity and delighted in exploiting the latest methods of communication. As congregations, audiences, and leaders

[26] Jonathan D. James (ed.), *A Moving Faith: Mega Churches Go South* (New Delhi, 2015).

in disparate locations became increasingly interactive and integrated, the prosperity gospel rapidly spread as a global phenomenon."[27] For those able to plot and document the transnational flows of influence and impact, "the key was networking and point-to-point contact." Bowler adeptly shows in her many networking charts of individuals, conferences, and locations just how thoroughly networked this prosperity gospel movement was and is in the lives of leading proponents like Oral Roberts, Kenneth Hagin, Carlton Pearson, and Marvin Winan.[28]

The principal means of dissemination of prosperity gospel theology has been through megachurches, first in the United States and now around the world. The cultural origins of the megachurch phenomenon in the Anglo-American world, what one historian has called "Big Religion," has a long history around urban concentrations of population, the evangelical imperative to ceaseless evangelism, and robust ideologies of growth and expansion built around faith in a divine command to be faithful and multiply.[29] More of a heterogeneous family of religious traditions than a straightforward teleology, megachurches in historical perspective have been associated with gilded age popular preachers, social gospelers,

---

[27] Kate Bowler, *Blessed: A History of the American Prosperity Gospel* (New York, 2013), 230–32.
[28] Bowler, *Blessed*, 84–85, 121, 185–86.
[29] Kip C. Richardson, "Big Religion: The Cultural Origins of the American Megachurch," Harvard University PhD (2017). Richardson locates the cultural origins of American megachurches further back into the nineteenth century than is conventionally assumed. He argues that the authorizing discourse is bigness itself, which acts as an inner theological motor driving the various cultural, denominational, and religious expressions.

revivalistic conservatives, Baptist fundamentalists, positive thinkers, and, increasingly, Pentecostal prosperity exponents. A primarily Anglo-American concept has now gone global, and the Global South is re-exporting it back to the Euro-American world through population migrations, church-planting, and a deliberate mission strategy. Its underpinning nucleus is a theology of Holy-Spirit-inspired "bigness" as demonstrable and irrefutable evidence of divine blessing. In this way, the size of churches and the size of their evangelistic ambition are sanctified as faith in the power of the Gospel message and of the enabling of the Holy Spirit.

The main growth hubs are cities in sub-Saharan Africa, Latin America, the Philippines, and South Korea, home of the world's largest church. Shared success stories and business models, international church growth conferences, circulating popular preachers, and ubiquitous praise music travel along the global networks. All gets amplified by a sophisticated deployment of social media, including television and radio, satellite TV and webcasting, social media and websites, and music and tape ministries. The scale is sometimes breathtaking. For example, in Lagos, Nigeria, two neighboring churches, The Redeemed Christian Church of God (RCCG) led by Enoch Adeboye and David O. Oyedepo's Living Faith Church Worldwide (LFCW), popularly known as the Winner's Chapel, have impressive multi-purpose sites and huge auditoriums. Adeboye's Redemption Camp and Oyedepo's Canaanland have all the facilities of a modern small town, and in the spirit of global extension another Redemption Camp is being planned for Floyd, a small town in northern Texas. There are many other megachurches with similar ambitions in Nigeria, and Nigerian pastors now lead the biggest single church in Western Europe, Kingsway International Christian Centre (KICC), based in London, which is affiliated to the RCCG, and a prominent megachurch in Kyiv in Eastern Europe. The missionary aspirations of these churches are equally grand. The RCCG aims to plant churches within five minutes' walk or driving distance in towns and cities throughout the world, and the Winner's Chapel has a network of more than three hundred churches in Nigeria and in more than sixty-three cities throughout Africa, the UK, and the USA.[30] The vision is to take the divine presence to all the nations of the world, thereby demonstrating the power of the Holy Spirit.[31] The possibilities are thought to be as endless as the spiritual power they embrace.

There is now a formidable African Christian diaspora back into Europe and North America made up of three major strands: branches of churches with mother church headquarters in Africa; churches formed directly by African migrants themselves; and "a proliferation of para-churches, prayer/fellowship groups and supportive or interdenominational ministries."[32] These African diaspora churches are often situated at nodal points of migration networks and self-consciously exploit network technologies in pursuit of their mission. They also build

[30] Walter C. Ihejirika and Godwin B. Okon, "Mega Churches and Megaphones: Nigerian Church Leaders and Their Media Ministries," in James, *A Moving Faith*, 62–82. See also Afe Adogame, *The African Christian Diaspora: New Currents and Emerging Trends in World Christianity* (London, 2013).
[31] Ihejirika and Okon, "Mega Churches and Megaphones," 73–78.
[32] Adogame, *The African Christian Diaspora*, 73–74.

ecumenical networks of churches, such as the Council of Christian Churches of an African Approach in Europe (CCCAAE) and the Scottish Council of African Churches (SCOAC), and promote networking through shared pulpits, expensive communication ventures, and large-scale international conferences. In this reverse pattern of migration and mission, not everything is plain sailing. Evangelistic strategies often morph from African-inspired interpersonal connections to more Western models of mass communication, and there are well-known tensions between churches with different lineages, whether Afro-Caribbean, African American, or African.[33] The African Christian diaspora reflects and exploits transnational movements of peoples propelled by globalization and novel communications media. Given current demographic trends, the African imprint on world Christianity, even in Europe and the United States, is going to increase in the century ahead.

One aspect of global networks of religious transmission that sometimes gets too little attention is music. The acknowledged primary worldwide hub, or node, in this network is Hillsong Church in Sydney, Australia. Founded in 1983, Hillsong was once affiliated with the Australian Assemblies of God but is now Australia's largest independent charismatic megachurch. In the words of one marketing expert, Hillsong Church "*de-religionized* organized religion into a spiritual product with its own brand."[34] Its best-selling product is its music label.

---

[33] Adogame, *The African Christian Diaspora*, 191–211.
[34] Jeaney Yip, "Marketing the Sacred: The Case of Hillsong Church, Australia," in James, *A Moving Faith*, 107.

Hillsong's praise and worship music has been recorded on dozens of albums, many of which have achieved gold or platinum status. Hillsong praise music has found its way into churches throughout the world, and in 2012 through the release of *The Global Project*, had a collection of its songs translated into nine languages. Hillsong Church now has five campuses in Australia, an extensive family of lucrative brand names, and satellite locations in London, Paris, Kiev, Cape Town, Stockholm, Moscow, Konstanz, New York, Amsterdam, and Copenhagen.[35] In an insightful analysis of the worship experience of the London branch of this transnational network, Tom Wagner states that this kind of congregational music is both "*a media object and a form of media*" that operates in a convergent and participatory culture "in which the lines between producer and consumer are blurred, where information is no longer *distributed*, but rather *circulated* in networks that (re)shape, (re)make, and (re)mix it to serve the personal and collective interests of its participants."[36] Ethnomusicologists tell us that music is a cultural system that helps mold human thought and emotions. In the history of Christian and congregational music, hymns and praise songs express personal relationship with the divine, create structures of meaning, and transform theological understandings. Whether it is the Lutheran hymns of the Protestant Reformation, the Wesleyan hymns of the evangelical Revival, or the praise songs of Hillsong, the

[35] Yip, "Marketing the Sacred," 106–26.
[36] Tom Wagner, "Music as a Mediated Object, Music as a Medium: Towards a Media Ecological View of Congregational Music," in Anna E. Nekola and Tom Wagner (eds.), *Congregational Music-Making and Community in a Mediated Age* (London, 2015), 25–44.

setting of words to music for congregational participation is perhaps the most influential and undervalued aspect of the transmission of religious meaning to mass audiences. In Hillsong praise music, as with Charles Wesley's hymns in an earlier era, there is a heavy use of personal pronouns in which the "intimacy of you and me introduces a spirit of closeness, warmth and approachability that is meant to communicate difference from the traditional stereotype of religion that denotes doctrines, authority, and rules."[37]

The worldwide dissemination of Hillsong praise music is somewhat reminiscent of the importance of Wesleyan hymns in the evangelical Revival, but there are also some significant differences. Although the Wesley brothers certainly used the best distribution networks available to them in disseminating the *Collection of Hymns* (1780) primarily to the people called Methodists, and although they appropriated popular tunes for added emotional cogency, John Wesley also exercised ruthless editorial and theological oversight and gave clear instructions about how, when, and where hymns should be sung to minimize the risk of emotional self-indulgence.[38] Through the application of new technologies and sophisticated international distribution and marketing networks, the Hillsong phenomenon is more self-consciously a brand, a product,

[37] Yip, "Marketing the Sacred," 112.
[38] David Hempton, *Methodism: Empire of the Spirit* (New Haven, 2005), 68–74. I write that Methodist hymns "supplied a poetic music of the heart for a religion of the heart. The medium and the message were in perfect harmony." For a fine analysis of the role of hymns in American religion, see Stephen Marini, "Hymnody as History: Early Evangelical Hymns and the Recovery of American Popular Religion," *Church History* 71 (June 2002), 273–306.

and an experience. The medium and the message are still indissolubly linked, but the whole Hillsong enterprise is even more indelibly marked by the cultural forces shaping it, namely, international corporate capitalism, experiential and therapeutic religion, transnational religious networks, the megachurch phenomenon, consumerist culture, and fast-moving technological changes in communications.

Just where all this might go was highlighted in a recent article in *The New York Times* entitled "Facebook Wants to Host Your Virtual Pew."[39] The reporter, Elizabeth Dias, writes, "Months before Hillsong opened its new outpost in Atlanta, its pastor sought advice on how to build a church in a pandemic. From Facebook." Facebook, which has more than three billion monthly users, more than the number of worldwide Christian adherents, is allegedly building connections with faith traditions as a way of building its brand and improving its reputation. Cheryl Sandberg, Facebook's Chief Operating Officer, is reported as saying, "Faith organizations and social media are a natural fit because fundamentally both are about connection. Our hope is that one day people will host religious services in virtual reality spaces as well, or use augmented reality as an educational tool to teach their children the story of their faith." What these connections between tech giants and global evangelical enterprises show is that each is making bets about the benefits of symbiotic relationships that will deliver market share and worldwide Christian growth, whether through conversions or virtual

---

[39] "Facebook Wants to Host Your Virtual Pew," *New York Times* (July 26, 2021), A12.

spirituality. The problem is that it is hard to know whether the beneficiaries will be known as customers, consumers, or congregants, or if it even makes much difference.

Given that we are all living through a period of rapid religious and cultural changes, it is not easy to estimate their long-term salience. Will these changes, which are partly inspired and facilitated by digital media and the internet, ultimately result in a religious revolution as profound as the one ushered in by print and Protestantism exactly five hundred years ago? In a controversial recent book by Joseph Henrich, an evolutionary biologist at Harvard, entitled *The Weirdest People in the World* (**W**estern, **E**ducated, **I**ndustrialized, **R**ich, and **D**emocratic), he makes a case for the central importance of the Lutheran Reformation in the evolution of the particular cultural and psychological characteristics of Western civilization. Luther himself was the product of three voluntary associations (a monk, in a university, in a charter town), and Henrich makes a compelling case for a causal relationship, not just an association, between Protestantism and increased literacy rates across Germany, Western Europe, and the wider world. Moreover, "broad-based literacy changed people's brains and altered their cognitive abilities in domains related to memory, visual processing, facial recognition, numerical exactness, and problem-solving."[40] He suggests that changes in family structure produced by medieval Christianity and the cultural processes unlocked by the Reformation, especially

[40] Joseph Henrich, *The Weirdest People in the World: How the West Became Psychologically Peculiar and Particularly Prosperous* (New York, 2020), 7–17 and 415–29.

increased literacy and information distribution, helped produce the WEIRD changes in Western culture. His main argument is that one cannot separate culture from psychology or psychology from biology because culture physically rewires our brains and thereby shapes how we think, which in turn reshapes culture. It is good to be clear that Henrich is not contending for some kind of innate racial categories and characteristics that somehow explain the rise of Western civilization, thereby endorsing its alleged superiority or rapaciousness. Rather, he presents compelling data to show that culture rewires our brains and the Lutheran Reformation was a major contributor, not just to religious change, but to cultural change capaciously understood.

If there is merit to that argument, what, then, might be said in a hundred years' time about the synergistic relationship between the digital revolution and religious and cultural change? I offer six possibilities for future discussion. The first is that the sheer speed, lack of regulation, and increased personal access of social media will accelerate the changes in Western Christianity that were already evident in the profound cultural shifts of the 1960s and 1970s. Second, there will be a continued weakening of traditional denominational Christianity, from both within and without. Within those denominations, social media professionals will increase their influence and theologians will have a diminished role. Institutions training future priests, pastors, and ministers, if they survive at all, will have to acknowledge that reality or risk going under. Third, Christianity will be impacted by both greater indigenization in the religious cultures of the Global South and increasing homogenization produced by transnational networks and other manifestations of globalization. It is possible that the tension between indigenized particularity and globalized homogeneity will be one of the most hotly debated topics of twenty-first-century Christianity. Fourth, individuals, especially those equipped to use social media, will continue to construct and find meaning in spiritualities designed by themselves or by networked cohorts with whom they choose to affiliate. Fifth, the social functions served by religion – quests for meaning and values, community connections and rituals, and spirituality and transcendence – will continue to be important and will inevitably produce continuity and change. If Joseph Henrich were to write a sequel in a hundred years' time about the relationship between religious, cultural, and psychological change in the early twenty-first century, my guess is that he could do worse than take courses in Nigerian Pentecostalism and the ethnomusicology of Hillsong. Alas for us, it is very unlikely that the significant action will have taken place at either Harvard or Edinburgh University Divinity Schools.

Finally, and perhaps most importantly, in the words of the Watergate investigation, is to follow the money. To go back to McLeod's delineation of Christian history into the three categories of the register, the ticket, and the website, these three epochs also have different financial models. The registering churches of medieval and early modern Christendom were largely financed by state-enforced ecclesiastical taxation in the form of tithes, church rates, and other financial exactions from populations who had to pay for religious establishments, whether they used them or not. The rise of British Nonconformity, Methodism, Baptists, and American non-establishment congregationalism, of all stripes, heralded not only new forms of religion, but also new financial models based on voluntary giving and donations, big and small. But the worldwide religious organizations of the postmodern era are financed on a different model. They expand their enterprises by product development, branding, marketing, and merchandizing. Where there is money there is also opportunity and growth, but there is also corruption and capitulation to the demands of the market.

The financing of religion has always been controversial and also deeply revealing about the location of power within religious traditions. In the Old Christendom model, established churches found themselves indissolubly linked to early modern political establishments on which they depended for their financial survival. When those political establishments were themselves challenged by new social forces, established churches found themselves representing interests perceived to be antithetical to those of their own parishioners. Throughout Western Europe, established churches paid a heavy price for their social and political loyalties in the age of revolutions from which they never fully recovered. Similarly, within new religious movements, such as Methodism, the original ideal of shared resources and egalitarian voluntary subscriptions eventually gave way to disproportionate influence exercised by the largest donors and the social forces they represented.[41] It is at least possible that the funding

[41] David Hempton, "A Tale of Preachers and Beggars: Methodism and Money in the Great Age of Transatlantic Expansion, 1780–1830," in Mark A. Noll (ed.), *God and Mammon: Protestants, Money, and the Market, 1790–1860* (New York, 2001), 123–46. The essays in this book make a powerful case for paying attention to the financing

models of the INC and megachurches discussed in this chapter, based as they are on products, marketing, and merchandising on the one hand and various forms of prosperity theology on the other, will raise expectations that cannot be delivered and keep producing leaders with little regulation of their prudence or probity.

The Lutheran Reformation progressed on the heels of an increasingly capitalistic printing industry, and over time produced increased literacy and the accumulation of cultural by-products of mass literacy. Five hundred years later, the digital revolution will transform the nature of global Christianity, from its funding models to its worship experiences, and from its community rituals to its information distribution. Big changes are already under way. What will be the balance sheet?

Here are three provisional perspectives. The first comes from the reflection of some theologians in the Zoom era, who are compelled to rethink church not as an institution with buildings and hierarchical orders, but of egalitarian and almost invisible communities connected by a desire for community even when bodies are not physically present. A second comes from *The Empathy Diaries* by Sherry Turkle, the Director of the MIT Initiative on Technology and Self. Her vision of the digital era is much more dystopian. "When we are online," she writes, "and when we are tracked by our devices our lives are bought

of religious enterprises and the cultural contexts in which they are embedded. See also David Hempton, "Organizing Concepts and 'Small Differences' in the Comparative Secularization of Western Europe and the United States," in David Hempton and Hugh McLeod (eds.), *Secularization and Religious Innovation in the North Atlantic World* (Oxford, 2017), 351–73.

and sold in bits and pieces to the highest bidder and for any purpose ... The social-media business model evolved to sell our privacy in ways that fracture both our intimacy and our democracy."[42] One might add that it has the capacity to fracture our empathy and our spirituality. A third perspective combines these possibilities in a way that will prove toxic to religion, by both eroding community and eradicating ritual, without which traditional forms of Christianity cannot easily survive. In the words of the South Korean philosopher Byung-Chul Han in his book, *The Disappearance of Rituals*, "Digital communication is increasingly developing into communication without community ... The so-called 'community' that is now invoked everywhere is an atrophied community, perhaps even a commodified and consumerized community. It lacks the symbolic power to bind people together."[43] Christianity shorn of its distinctive rituals and its capacity for fellowship will struggle to retain much of its historic attraction beyond the atomized loyalty of wired individuals.

---

[42] Sherry Turkle, *The Empathy Diaries: A Memoir* (New York, 2021), 337.
[43] Byung-Chul Han, *The Disappearance of Rituals: A Topology of the Present* (Cambridge, UK, 2020), 12–13.

Conclusion

～

Years ago, when I was a young professor at Queen's University Belfast during the infamous Troubles, the BBC asked me to contribute a radio lecture and book chapter to a new series it was producing on "The People of Ireland." The ostensible aim was to show that the people of Ireland were more diverse and variegated than the conventional "two traditions" narrative which many used as a framing device for interpreting the civil conflict in Northern Ireland. My assignment was to speak about religious minorities beyond the major Catholic and Protestant traditions. As I soon found out, these minorities were engagingly diverse and had complicated histories. Huguenots, Moravians, Palatines, Quakers, Methodists, Baptists, manifold nonconforming Presbyterian traditions, and others somehow made their way to Ireland, an off-shore island off an off-shore island, in early modern Europe. Of course, all of these traditions had their distinctive origin stories and had complex reasons for their geographical migrations and religious characteristics. In order to do justice to those factors, it was necessary to pay attention to underlying structures and conditions, including patterns of migration, the impact of war and religious persecution, economic and transportation networks, settlement patterns and natural topography, connections with religious contemporaries outside Ireland, and much else.[1] What took

[1] See Patrick Loughry (ed.), *The People of Ireland* (Belfast, 1988), 155–68.

me by surprise was the extent to which religious ideas and populations were more transnationally mobile than I had previously assumed and that the religious history of Ireland was more pluralistic than I had imagined.

The point of this story, and more capaciously the point of this book, is to show that when one pushes beyond the conventional paradigms of the history of Christianity – beyond highlighted events, religious hierarchies, institutions and denominations, national historiographies, and well-established analytical categories – into a more mobile and variegated world of what I have called nuclei, nodes, and networks, a different kind of light is shone on both familiar and unfamiliar stories and themes. To go back to my foundational metaphor, I have tried to construct a wild-garden version of the history of Christianity with undersoil connections that spread beyond established boundaries of nations and denominations. In this way, the perspective of both the gazer and what is seen is revolutionized, and new kinds of analytical categories emerge.

For example, building on the insight of the Pacific Islander scholar Epeli Hau'ofa (1939–2009),[2] who turned the outsider perspective of the Pacific Ocean as a vast sea of isolation and dislocation to an insider one of "Our Sea of Islands," Kirsty Murray has observed:

tracing networks is not just about identifying the organizations, individuals, or media pathways along which religious ideas may have travelled. It should also entail reflection on how connection and distance were perceived and understood by multiple actors. The insider and the outsider may describe individual

---

[2] Epeli Hau'ofa, *We Are the Ocean* (Honolulu, 2008), 27–40.

nodes and bonds as more or less significant. Local studies may reveal strong emotional investment in connections which seem insubstantial in another light. Perceptions of proximity and of distance, and of the very nature of networks, depends very much on where a person stands.[3]

She goes on to show how Pacific Islander women transmitted Christianity from island to island along with textile making, food preparation, and child-rearing practices in ways that missionary organizations did not initially intend. Moreover, some of this religious and cultural transmission across the island chain networks was financed by the contributions of British and American children who collected pennies and cents in their missionary boxes for mission ships for Melanesia. Moving back along the mission networks from periphery to metropole were stories of model conversions of Melanesian children, binding both senders and receivers into colonial and racialized perceptions of the Pacific Islands and their people. In this way, networks constructed by primarily white male explorers, conquerors, and missionaries were amplified and changed by women and children, and helped shape, popularize, and ultimately justify Western colonial projects.

The fact that this book emerged from a series of lectures which inevitably brought the writer into contact with a long-established node for the study of world Christianity in Edinburgh has also shaped its content. For most books there is an elongated period that leads from framing, writing, and publishing to garnering reviews,

---

[3] Kirsty Murray (2021), "Networks, Nodes and Nuclei Connecting the Study of World Christianity," Edinburgh Gifford Lectures Blog, https://tinyurl.com/3wuup4nt.

which often means that variegated feedback comes many years after the conceptualization of a project. Often the feedback is far too late and diffuse to have any influence on the way that the initial ideas are set afloat in the world through print media. Delivering the Gifford Lectures was different. After the delivery of each lecture there followed a vigorous question time and, in the spirit of modern technology, an active blog where students and professors posted expert comments in unscripted, egalitarian collaboration. The energy released is hard now to encapsulate in all its eclectic vigor. Ideas and criticisms came from all directions and from different disciplinary and spatial locations. For the lecturer, this process was both energizing and challenging as new spaces, both conceptual and geographical, were opened up. There was also the excitement of discovering that a particular method helped others see their own work in fresh ways. In that spirit, rather than writing a conventional conclusion about the main themes of my lectures, now book chapters, which should already be clear, I am choosing to present a kaleidoscope of reactions and suggestions which far outweigh any single person's capacity to respond. In that sense, these reactions are like the disseminating seeds of the wildflower spaces mentioned earlier. They have helped me see more clearly that in the stories I am telling, the social and spatial location of the gazer naturally determines the field of view. This is axiomatic, but in the field of religious history this simple truth has the capacity both to open up many new networks, nodes, and nuclei according to the location of the viewer and to increase the complexity of interpretations.

The most stimulating post-lecture questions and discussions operated around *four* different but linked sets of questions, which can serve as both conclusion and possible agenda for future work. The first had to do with the appropriate extent and limitations of networks and who should set the boundaries. Self-evidently, the less well-known networks created by the most marginalized, particularly lower-class women of color and Indigenous people at the outer edges of empires and religious traditions, are still the most under-researched and the least understood. Even with the best of intentions to rescue the participants in these networks from "the enormous condescension of posterity,"[4] the social and economic stratifications around gender, ethnicity, political power, and social status will mean that their stories will get told last.[5]

Another danger inherent in the approach taken in the preceding chapters is that so ubiquitous are networks in the forging of religious change, that "network theory" can be a convenient big tent within which everything is located, and nothing is eliminated. Questions, such as what the actual difference between a network and a movement is, or, more radically, what then is *not* a network, were understandably pressing. This was no mere posturing criticism. Anyone who has worked on the inner mechanisms of how established churches functioned in European Christendom knows very well that the inner

---

[4] This phrase is of course taken from E. P. Thompson, *The Making of the English Working Class* (London, 1968), 13.
[5] See the blog by Dr Katucha Bento, https://tinyurl.com/27s85zhc. She writes that 1888, the same year as the beginning of the Gifford Lecture series, was also the year that Brazil abolished slavery, which gave rise to "so many unofficial Black women's collectives who organized as a quilombo, favelas communities, marginalized neighborhoods (periferias) as they created ways to resist and refuse the places that the colonial-hegemonic society imposed on them."

structures of property and patronage networks were vital to their operation and survival. In everything, from the appointments of bishops and parish priests to the implementation of the legal system and the distribution of state propaganda, networks based on political loyalties, university connections, patronage, and local landowning structures played important roles in how the system worked. Religious hierarchies are also buttressed by networks.

The second set of questions that rose to the surface were those concerned with how to think better about the relationship between Christianity and empire in the early modern and modern world. As Ananya Chakravarti succinctly puts it, "There are good historical reasons why the contours of the global Church today are still largely indistinguishable from the erstwhile boundaries of Europe's empires."[6] There are obvious points to be made here that are well known. Indigenous peoples did not embrace Christianity, whatever that means from place to place, by imperial coercion alone, and the universal ambitions of both Catholic and Protestant Christians were related to, but not coterminous with, the expansionist drive for empire as an economic and cultural project. Chakravarti has herself shown how even the proto-ethnographic early Jesuit missionaries with their acknowledged sensitivity to their cultural surroundings helped produce the very hierarchical ethnographic schema of peoples, with Europeans at the top, that ultimately produced "a Eurocentric cartography of empire."[7] On the other hand, one blog on the

[6] Ananya Chakravarti, *The Empire of Apostles: Religion, Accommodatio, and the Imagination of Empire in Early Modern Brazil and India* (New Delhi, 2018), 4.
[7] Chakravarti, *The Empire of Apostles*, 10.

lecture dealing with global Pentecostalism wrote that it is possible to note the importance of events in the United States to the Pentecostal movements that emerged in Africa, Asia, and South America without making the latter derivative of the former. This writer urged avoidance of "the pitfalls of an uncritical post-colonialism. One which ironically denies agency to those it claims to 'liberate' by policing the boundaries of 'authenticity,' thereby acting as a form of governmentality no less invested in the management of 'native' subjectivities than the colonialism it ostensibly opposes."[8] This opinion nevertheless comes along with an acknowledgment that there is a kind of "epistemological power" bound up in the confluence of imperial and missionary projects which has the ability to shape the grammar and the concepts of both their supporters and opponents. Hence, the language and the conceptual apparatus used to interrogate empire are often used interchangeably for all aspects of colonialism – economic, religious, and political. Indeed, the language of empire is itself colonizing. While the history of Christian expansion and the rise of the European empires are inextricably linked, they are not always in synchronicity, in terms of either objectives or consequences.

A third set of questions operated around the well-known Marshal McLuhan quote about "the medium is the message."[9] Put another way, how did the various revolutions in communications along the way from the

---

[8] Nathan Dever, "Reflection: The Effectiveness of Applying Networks, Nodes and Nuclei to the Protestant International," https://tinyurl.com/mr2r84pp.

[9] Marshall McLuhan, *Understanding Media: The Extensions of Man* (New York, 1964).

print to the digital revolutions shape both the content of nuclei, the nature and location of nodes that became most important, and the ways in which networks expanded. As the American critic, Howard Rheingold, has observed, "People's social networks do not consist only of people they see face to face. In fact, social networks have been extending because of artificial media since the printing press and the telephone."[10] In evaluating how networks work, media and types of communications matter. Over time, these communications include many technological improvements to the speed and cost of print, railway and telegraph lines, steamships and new shipping routes, telephones and radio, movies and recordings, television and satellites, air travel and cell phones, and now social media of all kinds. More will come from the ever-increasing power of computers and Artificial Intelligence, which is already based on the predictive power of countless millions of networks way beyond the capacity of human brains to identify and analyze. A start has been made to show how many of the networks dealt with in this text were shaped by the media upon which they depended for mass transmission, but more needs to be done.[11] Horsfield's pioneering study, *From Jesus to the Internet: A History of Christianity and Media*, shows that

---

[10] *The New York Times*, February 16, 2000. See also Howard Rheingold, *Virtual Community: Homesteading on the Electronic Frontier* (New York, 1994).

[11] See, for example, Peter Horsfield, *From Jesus to the Internet: A History of Christianity and Media* (Chichester, West Sussex, 2015). For a geographically capacious treatment of networks and their cultural salience, see Manuel Castells (ed.), *The Network Society: A Cross-Cultural Perspective* (Cheltenham, UK, 2004), especially the Afterword by Rosalind Williams, "An Historian's View on the Network Society."

important though theological conflicts were to the history of Christianity, the spoils of victory went to those who most successfully used available media to disseminate their views. Moreover, the medium in which the message was contained inexorably shaped the message and the experience of recipients. In his study, "media and Christianity are revealed as symbiotic cultural phenomena." Throughout its remarkably diverse history, Christianity employed new media and technologies not simply as a tactic, but as both a conscious and unconscious adaptation to new "political, economic and cultural conditions." In that sense, Christianity and the networks it created were not delivering a fixed message in new forms, but were absorbing, reflecting and transmitting culturally modified and reconstructed forms of Christianity as "part of a much wider matrix of social and cultural changes."[12] Generally speaking, the closer the symbiosis between the medium and the message, the more "successful" the result, even as established elites within Christianity often bemoaned what they considered to be the pollution of the message. The most important point to be grasped here is that there was not just a single agreed-upon religious tradition called Christianity that happened to be spread by different technologies over time, but that both the cultural conditions in which new technologies were created and the technologies themselves inexorably changed and shaped the message itself.

Horsfield also shows that a large part of the success enjoyed by evangelicals and Pentecostals in the modern era was owing to how media-savvy minsters, preachers, and broadcasters adapted their messages to a growing

---

[12] Horsfield, *From Jesus to the Internet*, 288.

consumer market and new cultural expectations. One excellent example of how this worked is Marla Frederick's *Colored Television*, which charts how African American religious broadcasters and televangelists helped spread a message of prosperity and sexual redemption to women and men in the Caribbean Islands and throughout the world.[13] Health, purity, and prosperity were exported cultural products to populations whose social conditions were ripe for receiving them.

A fourth set of questions operated around the concepts of nuclei and nodes. How helpful is it to think of religious traditions capable of transnational mobility in terms of a religious nucleus with a particular DNA core? From Luther's Germany to Calvin's Geneva and from Wesley's Methodism to global Pentecostalism, what were the inner cores of ideas and practices that enabled these disparate religious traditions to grow and thrive thousands of miles from their points of origin? To ask that question is not to negate the importance of context, locale, and historical specificity in explaining how such traditions originated and established early footholds, but an overconcentration on those specificities and national traditions can lead to analytical categories too constrained by local or ideological particularities. The example I keep coming back to from my own academic career is how long it took me to break out from the very particular debates in British

---

[13] Marla F. Frederick, *Colored Television: American Religion Gone Global* (Stanford, 2016). Pentecostalism is also Africa's fastest growing form of Christianity. For an excellent recent treatment of spirit possession, sex, and deliverance in Accra, Ghana, see Nathanael J. Homewood, *Seductive Spirits: Deliverance, Demons, and Sexual Worldmaking in Ghanaian Pentecostalism* (Stanford, 2024).

history about whether or not Methodism helped save Britain from political revolution in the age of revolutions to consider how and why Methodism as primarily a woman's movement extended its reach to so many different parts of the world and eventually created its largest church in Seoul, South Korea.[14] The revolution question is not unimportant, but it tells you only so much about the lived experiences of countless millions of people far away from England's dark satanic mills which only ever accounted for a small minority of world Methodists.

The concept of nodal junction boxes in religious transmission is also worthy of greater study. Some, such as London's Fetter Lane Society in the history of the First Great Awakening or Azusa Street in the origins of Pentecostalism, are both obvious and dangerous in possibly explaining too much. But other kinds of junction boxes are clearly important in the transmission of religious traditions. Universities, cities, communication hubs, conferences, and unforeseeable collisions based on population movements all show up in this text as important locations not only for constructing new religious traditions, but also in generating energy and opportunity for their expansion. Some of these nodes are obvious and privilege social and educational elites, but some of the most influential operate at social levels not always well covered by historians, do not show up in traditional archives, and still remain to be uncovered.

Ultimately, the worthwhileness of the concepts of networks, nodes, and nuclei as applied to the wilder gardens

---

[14] For an insider account of the Kwanglim Church in Korea, see Kim Sundo, *A Miracle of Five Minutes* (Nashville, 2015).

of the history of Christianity depends, like any other theory or method, on whether it expands the discourse, advances knowledge, and captures the energy of dynamic transformation. In other words, does it supply better explanations for some of the religious developments we already know something about along with others that we have only a dim understanding of, or no understanding at all? My hope for the 2021 Gifford Lectures, now in print as *Christianity at the Crossroads*, is that they pass this pragmatic utilitarian test without introducing new interpretative ghosts into the machine.

SELECT BIBLIOGRAPHY

This is a selection of the most important books cited in the text. For details about other materials cited in the text, such as journal articles and contemporary sources, please follow the footnotes in the text.

Adogame, A., *The African Christian Diaspora: New Currents and Emerging Trends in World Christianity* (London, 2013)

Akenson, D. H., *Discovering the End of Time: Irish Evangelicals in the Age of Daniel O'Connell* (Montreal & Kingston, 2016)

Akenson, D. H., *Exporting the Rapture: John Nelson Darby and the Victorian Conquest of North American Evangelicalism* (New York, 2018)

Anderson, A. H., *An Introduction to Pentecostalism* (Cambridge, 2004)

Anderson, A. H., *To the Ends of the Earth: Pentecostalism and the Transformation of Global Christianity* (Oxford, 2013)

Anderson, E., *The Betrayal of Faith: The Tragic Journey of a Colonial Native Convert* (Cambridge, MA, 2007)

Anderson, E., *The Death and Afterlife of the North American Martyrs* (Cambridge, MA, 2013)

Anderson, R. M., *Vision of the Disinherited: The Making of American Pentecostalism* (New York, 1979)

Andrews, D. E., *The Methodists and Revolutionary America, 1760–1800: The Shaping of an Evangelical Culture* (Princeton, 2000)

Atkins, G., *Converting Britannia: Evangelicals and British Public Life, 1770–1840* (Woodbridge, Suffolk, 2019)

Balmer, R., *Evangelicalism in America* (Waco, TX, 2016)

Bebbington, D. W., *The Dominance of Evangelicalism: The Age of Spurgeon and Moody* (Downers Grove, IL, 2005)

Benedict, P., *Christ's Churches Purely Reformed: A Social History of Calvinism* (New Haven, 2002)

Bergunder, M., Droogers, A., and Laan, C. V. (eds), *Studying Global Pentecostalism: Theories and Methods* (Berkeley, 2010)

Black, J., *British Politics and Society from Walpole to Pitt 1742–1789* (London, 1990)

Blumhofer, E. L., *Aimee Semple McPherson: Everybody's Sister* (Grand Rapids, MI, 1993)

Blythe, C., *Terrible Revolution: Latter-Day Saints and the American Apocalypse* (New York, 2020)

Boerl, C. W. and Donbavand, K., *A God More Powerful Than Yours: American Evangelicals, Politics, and the Internet Age* (Newcastle upon Tyne, 2015)

Bowler, K., *Blessed: A History of the American Prosperity Gospel* (New York, 2013)

Bowler, K., *The Preacher's Wife: The Precarious Power of Evangelical Women Celebrities* (Princeton, 2019).

Brekus, C. A., *Sarah Osborn's World: The Rise of Evangelical Christianity in Early America* (New Haven, 2013)

Brekus, C. A., *Strangers & Pilgrims: Female Preaching in America, 1740–1845* (Chapel Hill, NC, 1998)

Breward I., *A History of the Churches in Australasia* (Oxford, 2001)

Brewitt-Taylor, S., *Christian Radicalism in the Church of England and the Invention of the British Sixties, 1957–1970: The Hope of a World Transformed* (Oxford, 2018)

Brown, C. B., *Singing the Gospel: Lutheran Hymns and the Success of the Reformation* (Cambridge, MA, 2005)

Brown, C. G., *The Death of Christian Britain* (London, 2001)

Brown, C. G. and Snape, M. (eds), *Secularisation in the Christian World* (Farnham, Surrey, 2010)

Brusco, E. E., *The Reformation of Machismo: Evangelical Conversion and Gender in Colombia* (Austin, TX, 1995)

Burin, E., *Slavery and the Peculiar Solution: A History of the American Colonization Society* (Gainesville, FL, 2005)

Burns, K., *Colonial Habits: Convents and the Spiritual Economy of Cuzco, Peru* (Durham, NC, 1999)

Butler, A., *Women in the Church of God in Christ: Making a Sanctified World* (Chapel Hill, NC, 2007)

Byrd, A. X., *Captives and Voyagers: Black Migrants across the Eighteenth-Century British Atlantic World* (Baton Rouge, LA, 2008)

Byrne, J., *The Other Catholics: Remaking America's Largest Religion* (New York, 2016)

Campbell, H., *Exploring Religious Community Online: We Are One in the Network* (New York, 2005)

Campbell, H. A., *Digital Creatives and the Rethinking of Religious Authority* (New York, 2021)

Campbell, H. A., *When Religion Meets New Media* (London, 2010)

Campbell, H. A. and Garner, S., *Networked Theology: Negotiating Faith in Digital Culture* (Grand Rapids, MI, 2016)

Carey, W., *An Enquiry into the Obligations of Christians, to Use Means for the Conversion of the Heathens. In which the Religious State of the Different Nations of the World, the Success of Former Undertakings, and the Practicability of Further Undertakings Are Considered* (Leicester, 1792)

Carté, K., *Religion and the American Revolution: An Imperial History* (Chapel Hill, NC, 2021)

Chakravarti, A., *The Empire of Apostles: Religion, Accommodatio, and the Imagination of Empire in Early Modern Brazil and India* (New Delhi, 2018)

Chilcote, P. W. (ed.), *Her Own Story: Autobiographical Portraits of Early Methodist Women* (Nashville, TN, 2001)

Christerson, B. and Flory, R., *The Rise of Network Christianity: How Independent Leaders Are Changing the Religious Landscape* (New York, 2017)

Clark, E., *Masterless Mistresses: The New Orleans Ursulines and the Development of a New World Society, 1727–1834* (Chapel Hill, NC, 2007)

Coad, F. R., *A History of the Brethren Movement: Its Origins, Its Worldwide Development, and Its Significance for the Present Day* (Exeter, 1968)

Cornell, D., *American Madonna: Crossing Borders with the Virgin Mary* (Maryknoll, NY, 2010)

Cott, N., *Bonds of Womanhood: "Woman's Sphere" in New England, 1780–1835* (New Haven, 1977)

Cox, H., *Fire from Heaven: The Rise of Pentecostal Spirituality and the Reshaping of Religion in the Twenty-first Century* (New York, 1995)

Davis, K., *Periodization and Sovereignty: How Ideas of Feudalism and Secularization Govern the Politics of Time* (Philadelphia, 2008)

Dixon, C. S., *Protestants: A History from Wittenberg to Pennsylvania* (Chichester, West Sussex, 2010)

Du Mez, K. K., *Jesus and John Wayne: How White Evangelicals Corrupted a Faith and Fractured a Nation* (New York, 2020)

Edwards, M. U., *Printing, Propaganda, and Martin Luther* (Berkeley, 1994)

Eliot, G., *Essays and Leaves from a Note-Book* (London, 1884)

Evans, S. M. (ed.), *Journeys that Opened Up the World: Women, Student Christian Movements, and Social Justice, 1955–1975* (Piscataway, NJ, 2003)

Everill, B., *Abolition and Empire in Sierra Leone and Liberia* (Basingstoke, 2013)

Fenn, R. K. (ed.), *The Blackwell Companion to the Sociology of Religion* (Oxford, 2003)

Ferguson, N., *The Square and the Tower: Networks and Power, from the Freemasons to Facebook* (New York, 2018)

Field, C. D., *Secularization in the Long 1960s: Numerating Religion in Britain* (Oxford, 2017)

Fitzgerald, F., *The Evangelicals: The Struggle to Shape America* (New York, 2017)

Frederick, M. F., *Colored Television: American Religion Gone Global* (Stanford, 2016)

Friedman, B. M., *Religion and the Rise of Capitalism* (New York, 2021)

Friedrich, M., *The Jesuits: A History* (Princeton, 2022)

Ganss, G. E., S. J. (ed.), *The Spiritual Exercises of Saint Ignatius* (Chicago, 1992)

Gates Jr., H. L., *The Black Church: This Is Our Story, This Is Our Song* (New York, 2021)

Goldstein, J. (ed.), *Foucault and the Writing of History* (Oxford, 1994)

Gordon, G., *From Slavery to Freedom: The Life of David George, Pioneer Black Baptist Minister* (Hansport, Nova Scotia, 1992)

Gregory, B. S., *The Unintended Reformation: How a Religious Revolution Secularized Society* (Cambridge, MA, 2012)

Griffith, R. M., *God's Daughters: Evangelical Women and the Power of Submission* (Berkeley, 1997)

Hackett, D. G., *That Religion in which All Men Agree: Freemasonry in American Culture* (Berkeley, 2014)

Hägerstrand, T., *Innovation Diffusion as a Spatial Process* (Chicago, 1967)

Hall, D. D., *The Puritans: A Transatlantic History* (Princeton, 2019)

Han, B.-C., *The Disappearance of Rituals: A Topology of the Present* (Cambridge, UK, 2020)

Hankins, B. (ed.), *Evangelicalism and Fundamentalism: A Documentary Reader* (New York, 2008)

Hastings, A., *The Construction of Nationhood: Ethnicity, Religion and Nationalism* (Cambridge, 1997)

Hatch, N., *The Democratization of American Christianity* (New Haven, 1989)

Hatch, N. O., *The Democratization of American Christianity* (New Haven, 1989)

Hau'ofa, E., *We Are the Ocean* (Honolulu, HI, 2008)

Hempton, D., *Evangelical Disenchantment: Nine Portraits of Faith and Doubt* (New Haven, 2008)

Hempton, D., *Methodism: Empire of the Spirit* (New Haven, 2005)

Hempton, D., *The Church in the Long Eighteenth Century* (London, 2011)

Hempton, D. and McLeod, H., *Secularization and Religious Innovation in the North Atlantic World* (Oxford, 2017)

Henold, M. J., *Catholic and Feminist: The Surprising History of the American Catholic Movement* (Chapel Hill, NC, 2008)

Henrich, J., *The Weirdest People in the World: How the West Became Psychologically Peculiar and Particularly Prosperous* (New York, 2020)

Higginbotham, E. B., *Righteous Discontent: The Women's Movement in the Black Baptist Church, 1880–1920* (Cambridge, MA, 1993)

Hill, K., *Baptism, Brotherhood, and Belief in Reformation Germany: Anabaptism and Lutheranism, 1525–1585* (Oxford, 2015)

Homewood, N. J., *Seductive Spirits: Deliverance, Demons, and Sexual Worldmaking in Ghanaian Pentecostalism* (Stanford, 2024)

Hoover, S. M., *Religion in the Media Age* (New York, 2006)

Horne, M., *Letters on Missions; Addressed to the Protestant Ministers of British Churches* (Bristol, 1794)

Horsfield, P. G., *From Jesus to the Internet: A History of Christianity and Media* (Chichester, West Sussex, 2015)

Howe, D. W., *What God Hath Wrought: The Transformation of America, 1815–1848* (New York, 2007)

Hummel, D. G., *The Rise and Fall of Dispensationalism: How the Evangelical Battle over the End Times Shaped a Nation* (Grand Rapids, MI, 2023)

Jackson, M. O., *The Human Network: How Your Social Position Determines Your Power, Beliefs, and Behaviors* (New York, 2019)

James, J. D. (ed.), *A Moving Faith: Mega Churches Go South* (New Delhi, 2015)

Jasanoff, M., *Liberty's Exiles: American Loyalists in the Revolutionary World* (New York, 2011)

Johnson, S. A., *African American Religions, 1500–2000: Colonialism, Democracy and Freedom* (New York, 2015)

Kalu, O., *African Pentecostalism: An Introduction* (New York, 2008)

Kanter, D. E., *Chicago Catolico: Making Catholic Parishes Mexican* (Chicago, 2020)

Kaplan, B. J., *Divided by Faith: Religious Conflict and the Practice of Toleration in Early Modern Europe* (Cambridge, MA, 2007)

Keller, R. S. and Ruether, R. R. (eds), *Encyclopedia of Women and Religion in North America*, vol. 2 (Bloomington, IA, 2006)

Kim, H., *Race for Revival: How Cold War South Korea Shaped the American Evangelical Empire* (New York, 2022)

Krebs, J. M., *Our Lady of Emmitsburg, Visionary Culture, and Catholic Identity: Seeing and Believing* (Lanham, MD, 2016)

Kuile, C. T., *The Power of Ritual: Turning Everyday Activities into Soulful Practices* (New York, 2020)

Leary, M. R., *The Curse of the Self: Self Awareness, Egotism, and the Quality of Human Life* (New York, 2004)

Lian, X., *Redeemed by Fire: The Rise of Popular Christianity in Modern China* (New Haven, 2010)

Loughry, P. (ed.), *The People of Ireland* (Belfast, 1988)

Lyerly, C. L., *Methodism and the Southern Mind, 1770–1810* (New York, 1998)

Mack, P., *Heart Religion in the British Enlightenment: Gender and Emotion in Early Methodism* (Cambridge, 2008)

Mahmood, S., *Politics of Piety: The Islamic Revival and the Feminist Subject* (Princeton, 2012)

Marsden, G. M., *Understanding Fundamentalism and Evangelicalism* (Grand Rapids, MI, 1991)

Martin, D., *Pentecostalism: The World Their Parish* (Oxford, 2002)

Mason, J. C. S., *The Moravian Church and the Missionary Awakening in England 1760–1800* (London, 2001)

Matovina, T., *Latino Catholicism: Transformation in America's Largest Church* (Princeton, 2012)

Maxwell, D., *African Gifts of the Spirit: Pentecostalism & the Rise of a Zimbabwean Transnational Religious Movement* (Oxford, 2006)

McDannell, C., *Sister Saints: Mormon Women since the End of Polygamy* (New York, 2019)

McGreevy, J. T., *American Jesuits and the World: How an Embattled Religious Order Made Modern Catholicism Global* (Princeton, 2016)

McGreevy, J. T., *Catholicism: A Global History from the French Revolution to Pope Francis* (New York, 2022)

McLeod, H., *The Religious Crisis of the 1960's* (Oxford, 2007)

McLeod, H. and Ustorf, W. (eds), *The Decline of Christendom in Western Europe, 1750–2000* (Cambridge, 2003)

McLuhan, M., *Understanding Media: The Extensions of Man* (New York, 1964)

McShea, B., *Apostles of Empire: The Jesuits and New France* (Lincoln, NE, 2019)

Miller, P., *Good Catholics: The Battle over Abortion in the Catholic Church* (Berkeley, 2014)

Mills, B., *The World Colonization Made: The Racial Geography of Early American Empire* (Philadelphia, 2020)

Mills, K., Taylor, W. B., and Graham, S. L. (eds), *Colonial Latin America: A Documentary History* (Lanham, MD, 2004)

Morgan, D., *Protestants and Pictures: Religion, Visual Culture, and the Age of American Mass Production* (New York, 1999)

Neilson, R. L. and Woods, F. E., *Go Ye Into All the World: The Growth and Development of Mormon Missionary Work* (Provo, UT, 2012)

Nekola, A. E. and Wagner, T. (eds), *Congregational Music-Making and Community in a Mediated Age* (London, 2015)

Noll, M. A. (ed.), *God and Mammon: Protestants, Money, and the Market, 1790–1860* (New York, 2001)

Noll, M. A., *A History of Christianity in the United States and Canada* (Grand Rapids, MI, 1992)

Noll, M. A., *In the Beginning Was the Word: The Bible in American Public Life, 1492–1783* (New York, 2016)

O'Malley, J. W., Bailey, G. A., Harris, S. J., and Kennedy, T. F. (eds), *The Jesuits: Cultures, Sciences, and the Arts, 1540–1773* (Toronto, 1999) and *The Jesuits II: Cultures, Sciences, and the Arts, 1540–1773* (Toronto, 2006)

Orsi, R. A., *History and Presence* (Cambridge, MA, 2016)

Orsi, R. A., *The Madonna of 115th Street: Faith and Community in Italian Harlem, 1880–1950* (New Haven, 2002)

Otis, L., *Networking: Communicating with Bodies and Machines in the Nineteenth Century* (Ann Arbor, MI, 2001)

Owens, S. E., *Nuns Navigating the Spanish Empire* (Albuquerque, 2017)

Peña, E. L., *Performing Piety: Making Sacred Space with the Virgin of Guadalupe* (Berkeley, 2011)

Petrey, T. G. and Hoyt, A. (eds), *The Routledge Handbook of Mormonism and Gender* (Milton, 2020)

Pettegree, A., *Brand Luther* (London, 2016)

Putnam, R. D. and Campbell, D. E., *American Grace: How Religion Divides and Unites Us* (New York, 2010)

Rawlyk, G. A., *The Canada Fire: Radical Evangelicalism in British North America 1775–1812* (Kingston and Montreal, 1994)

Reeves-Ellington, B., Sklar, K. K., and Shemo, C. A. (eds), *Competing Kingdoms: Women, Mission, Nation, and the American Protestant Empire, 1812–1960* (Durham, NC, 2010)

Rheingold, H., *Virtual Community: Homesteading on the Electronic Frontier* (New York, 1994)

Robeck, Jr., C. M., *The Azusa St Mission & Revival: The Birth of the Global Pentecostal Movement* (Nashville, TN, 2006)

Robeck, Jr., C. M. and Young, A. (eds), *The Cambridge Companion to Pentecostalism* (New York, 2014)

Robert, D. L., *American Women in Mission: A Social History of Their Thought and Practice* (Macon, GA, 1997)

Robert, D. L., *Christian Mission: How Christianity became a World Religion* (Chichester, West Sussex, 2009)

Robert, D. L. and Bearers, G., *Gender Barriers: Missionary Women in the Twentieth Century* (Maryknoll, NY, 2002)

Roof, W. C., *Spiritual Marketplace: Baby Boomers and the Remaking of American Religion* (Princeton, 1999)

Ross, A. C., *A Vision Betrayed: The Jesuits in Japan and China, 1542–1742* (Maryknoll, NY, 1994)

Rowdon, H. H., *The Origins of the Brethren 1825–1850* (London, 1967)

Sandeen, E. R., *The Roots of Fundamentalism: British and American Millenarianism, 1800–1930* (Chicago, 1970)

Sanders, C. J., *Saints in Exile: The Holiness-Pentecostal Experience in African American Religion and Culture* (New York, 1996)

Sanneh, L., *Abolitionists Abroad: American Blacks and the Making of Modern West Africa* (Cambridge, MA, 1999)

Sanneh, L., *Disciples of All Nations: Pillars of World Christianity* (Oxford, 2008)

Schlenther, B. S., *Queen of the Methodists: The Countess of Huntingdon and the Eighteenth-Century Crisis of Faith and Society* (Durham, UK, 1997)

Schmidt, J. M., *Grace Sufficient: A History of Women in American Methodism, 1760–1939* (Nashville, TN, 1999)

Schneider, A. G., *The Way of the Cross Leads Home: The Domestication of American Methodism* (Bloomington, IA, 1993)

Sciorra, J., *Built with Faith: Italian American Imagination and Catholic Material Culture in New York City* (Chicago, 2015)

Scribner, B., Porter, R., and Teich, M. (eds), *The Reformation in National Context* (Cambridge, 1994)

Sensbach, J., *Rebecca's Revival: Creating Black Christianity in the Atlantic World* (Cambridge, MA, 2005)

Sewell, W. H., *Logics of History: Social Theory and Social Transformation* (Chicago, 2005)

Shyllon, L. T., *Two Centuries of Christianity in an African Province of Freedom: Sierra Leone, A Case Study of European Influence and Culture in Church Development* (Freetown, Sierra Leone, 2008)

Spangenberg, A. G., *An Account of the Manner in which the Protestant Church of the Unitas Fratum, or United Brethren, Preach the Gospel and Carry on their Missions among the Heathen* (London, 1788)

Stephens, R., *The Fire Spreads: Holiness and Pentecostalism in the American South* (Cambridge, MA, 2010)

Sundo, K., *A Miracle of Five Minutes* (Nashville, TN, 2015)

Sutton, M. A., *American Apocalypse: A History of Modern Evangelicalism* (Cambridge, MA, 2014)

Taylor, W. B., *Shrines and Miraculous Images: Religious Life in Mexico Before the Reforma* (Albuquerque, 2010)

Taylor, W. B., *Theater of a Thousand Wonders: A History of Miraculous Images and Shrines in New Spain* (New York, 2016)
Thomas, T., *Kincraft: The Making of Black Evangelical Sociality* (Durham, NC and London, 2021)
Turkle, S., *The Empathy Diaries: A Memoir* (New York, 2021)
Tweed, T. A. (ed.), *Retelling U.S. Religious History* (Berkeley, 1997)
Tweed, T. A., *Our Lady of the Exile: Diasporic Religion at a Cuban Catholic Shrine in Miami* (New York, 1997)
Tyler-McGraw, M., *An African Republic: Black and White Virginians in the Making of Liberia*
Vaca, D., *Evangelicals Incorporated: Books and the Business of Religion in America* (Cambridge, MA, 2019)
Wacker, G., *Heaven Below: Early Pentecostals and American Culture* (Cambridge, MA, 2001)
Walker, J. W. St. G., *The Black Loyalists: The Search for a Promised Land in Nova Scotia and Sierra Leone, 1783–1870* (Toronto, 1993)
Walls, A. F., *The Cross- Cultural Process in Christian History* (Maryknoll, NY, 2002)
Walls, A. F., *The Missionary Movement in Christian History: Studies in the Transmission of Faith* (Maryknoll, NY, 1996)
Ward, W. R., *Christianity under the Ancien Régime 1648–1789* (Cambridge, 1999)
Ward, W. R., *Early Evangelicalism: A Global Intellectual History, 1670–1789* (Cambridge, 2006)
Ward, W. R., *Faith and Faction* (London, 1993)
Ward, W. R., *Religion and Society in England, 1790–1850* (London, 1972)
Weisenfeld, J., *African American Women and Christian Activism: New York's Black YMCA, 1905–1945* (Cambridge, MA, 1998)
Wertheim, M., *The Pearly Gates of Cyberspace: A History of Space from Dante to the Internet* (New York, 1999)
Wolffe, J., *The Expansion of Evangelicalism: The Age of Wilberforce, More, Chalmers and Finney* (Downers Grove, IL, 2007)

Worcester, T. (ed.), *The Cambridge Companion to the Jesuits* (Cambridge, 2008)

Wuthnow, R., *Boundless Faith: The Global Outreach of American Churches* (Berkeley, 2009)

Zimdars-Swartz, S. L., *Encountering Mary: Visions of Mary from La Salette to Medjugorje* (Princeton, 1991)

Zupanov, I. G. (ed.), *The Oxford Handbook of the Jesuits* (New York, 2019)

INDEX

American Madonna: Crossing
Borders with the Virgin
Mary (Cornell), 88
American Moravianism, 35
American Protestant
missionaries, 155
American Revolutionary War,
36, 92, 93, 94, 100, 109
American Society of Jesus, 33
American Women in Mission:
A Social History of Their
Thought and Practice
(Robert), 142
An Account of the Manner
in which the Protestant
Church of the Unitas
Fratum, or United
Brethren, Preach the
Gospel, and Carry
on their Missions
among the Heathen
(Spangenberg), 118
An African Republic: Black and
White Virginians in the
Making of Liberia (Tyler-
McGraw), 105
An Enquiry into the Obligations
of Christians, to Use Means
for the Conversion of the
Heathens (Carey), 119
An Introduction to
Pentecostalism
(Anderson), 140
Anabaptists/Anabaptism, 57
Anderson, A. H., 136, 137,
140, 152
Andrews, D. E., 15, 151
Anglican Communion Online,
184
Anglicanism, 16
anti-sectarianism, 42
anti-Aristotelianism, 115
anti-Catholicism, 23, 54, 150, 167

antinomianism, 135
The Anxious Generation: How
the Great Rewiring of
Childhood Is Causing of
Mental Illness (Haidt), 180
apocalypticism, 121, 122, 125, 130
Apostles, 100
Apostles of Empire:
The Jesuits and New
France (McShea), 64
The Apostolic Faith (Seymour),
139
Archdiocese of Chicago, 84
Art, Controversy, and the
Jesuits: The Imago Primi
Saeculi (O'Malley), 67
Artificial Intelligence, 216
Arulappan, J. C., 137
Atkins, G., 90, 91, 92, 96, 119
Azusa Street revival, 13, 36, 96,
136, 137, 138, 139, 140,
141, 219
The Azusa St Mission & Revival:
The Birth of the Global
Pentecostal Movement
(Robeck), 139, 140

Bailey, G. A., 59
Balmer, R., 132
Bank of England, 90
baptism, 99
Holy Spirit, 133, 139, 141,
144, 153
*Baptism, Brotherhood, and Belief
in Reformation Germany:
Anabaptism and Lutheranism*
(Hill), 58
*The Baptism of the Holy Ghost &
Fire* (Abrams), 141
Baptist Missionary Society, 117
Baptists, 98, 117, 176, 197,
205, 209
evangelicalism, 93

Index

Index

239

Index

Index

Harrison, J. E., xi
Harvard Divinity School, 189
Harvest Network, 38
Hastings, A., 52
Hat and Cloak Riots, 70
Hatch, N. O., 37, 112
Hau'ofa, E., 210
Heart Religion in the British Enlightenment: Gender and Emotion in Early Methodism (Mack), 151
A Heart-Shaped World: Jesuit Consolation Culture in a Globalizing World, 1500–1800 (Molina), 61
Heaven Below: Early Pentecostals and American Culture (Wacker), 133
Hebrew Bible, 126, 153
Hempton, D., 15, 31, 69, 110, 111, 151, 182, 201, 206, 207
Henold, M. J., 168, 171
Henrich, J., 203
Her Own Story: Autobiographical Portraits of Early Methodist Women (Chilcote), 151
Herodotus, 3
Higginbotham, E. B., 175
Hill, K., 58
Hillsong Church, 199, 200, 202
praise songs of, 200
History and Presence (Orsi), 86
A History of Christianity in the United States and Canada (Noll), 132
A History of the Brethren Movement: Its Origins, Its Worldwide Development, and Its Significance for the Present Day (Roy Coad), 126
A History of the Churches in Australasia (Breward), 15
Holiness movement, 37, 138, 139

Holy Church of Austerlitz, 57
Holy Ghost baptism. *See* Holy Spirit baptism
Holy Roman Empire, 59
Holy Spirit, 197, 198
Holy Spirit baptism, 133, 139, 141, 144, 153
Homewood, N. J., 218
Hoover, S. M., 191
Horae Apocalypticae (Elliott), 128
Horne, M., 119
Horsfield, P. G., 216, 217
How We Gather (Thurston and Kuile), 190
Howe, D. W., 112
Hoyt, A., 160
Hufton, O., 61, 66
Hughes, J. S., 87
The Human Network: How your Social Position Determines your Power, Beliefs, and Behaviors (Jackson), 27
Hummel, D. G., 121, 124, 127
Hymnody as History: Early Evangelical Hymns and the Recovery of American Popular Religion (Marini), 201
hymns, 47, 50, 128
Charles Wesley, 201
Martin Luther, 51, 200
printing, 50
of sixteenth century, 51
writing, 114

Iberian, 76, 78, 106, 165, 166
Catholicism, 34, 80
discoverers and conquerors, network of, 7, 29, 45
Ignatius of Loyola, 59, 65, 67
Jesuit organization, 68
organizational talents of, 65
schools and colleges of, 81

Index